Love, Laughter, and Morphine

BOOKS BY TORIE COOPER

Nature:
A Collection of Poems

Laying Nana Down:
Poems of Caregiving and Loss

Love, Laughter, and Morphine

*A Compassionate Guide for Caregivers
of the Terminally Ill*

Torie Cooper

Blue Wattle Press

Cover Illustration: © Torie Cooper

Copyright © 2019 Torie Cooper
All rights reserved
ISBN-13: 978-0-9990856-2-2

All photos courtesy of the author, with the following exception: page 216, The Author with her Grandmother: Valerie Bowen

*In Loving Memory of
Joyce Hicks*

*Mother, Grandmother,
and Great-Grandmother.*

Disclaimer
This book is not a substitute for advice or treatment from Palliative Care professionals.

Table of Contents

Introduction . xiii

CHAPTER 1 - First Steps on a Long Road . 19
A Brief Overview of Caregiving . 20
It's Normal to Feel Overwhelmed and Upset . 22
Be Ready to Make Mistakes . 23
Preparation for Caregiving . 23
Sleep Deprivation . 24
Monitor Your Loved One . 25
Take Breaks While You Can . 26
Relationships Issues . 27
Encourage Open Communication . 28
The Nursing Home Discussion . 29
Accept and Seek Assistance . 31
Share the Care . 31
Spiritual Considerations . 32
Maintain a Routine for Your Loved One . 32
Mindfulness . 33
Use of Humor . 34
Practical Tips . 35

CHAPTER 2 – You the Caregiver: No Batteries, Love Powered . 51
Emotions and Stress . 52
The Relationship Between You and Your Loved One . 55
Monitor Your Own Well-Being . 56
Making Mistakes . 58
Balancing Communication with Family and Friends . 59
Divided Days and Quality Time . 60
Leaving Your Brain Behind . 60
Grief Begins Prior to Death . 63
Supermarket Holiday . 64
Life Happens While Caregiving . 65
Caregiver's Guilt . 66
Practical Tips . 66
Conversation Starters . 70

CHAPTER 3 – Your Terminally Ill Loved One . 77
Transformation is the New Normal . 78
Awareness of Death . 79
Relationship in the Midst of Illness . 80
Mental Confusion . 81
Let Your loved one Care for You . 83
Not Wanting to be a Bother . 84
Food Issues . 85
Spiritual Considerations . 87
Be a Medical Monitor . 88
Awkward Situations . 89
Surprise Your Loved One . 90
Allow Your Loved One to Exercise Control . 91
Celebrate Important Occasions . 92
Use Humor . 93
Practical Tips . 94
Conversation Starters . 95

CHAPTER 4 - Family and Friends . 101
  Family and Friends Need Time with Their Loved One . 102
  Allow Family and Friends to Give You a Break . 103
  Family and Friends are 'One of Many' . 103
  Concerns Regarding Food and Beverage . 104
  Relationship Issues . 105
  When Family and Friends Choose Not to Visit . 106
  Caregiving Skills – Helpful Critique or Criticism? . 107
  Chat, Laugh, and Entertain . 108
  Managing Telephone Calls . 109
  Lend Your Ear . 110
  Food Storage Issues . 111
  Conversation Starters . 111

CHAPTER 5 – The Palliative Care Team and Other Supporters . 119
  Education and Communication . 120
  Community Nursing Services . 121
  Maintain Good Relationships . 122
  What is Palliative Care? . 122
  Doctors and Nurses . 123
  Social Workers . 123
  Occupational Therapists . 124
  Pastoral Care . 124
  Volunteers . 124
  Paramedics . 125
  The Night the Cavalry Came . 125
  Conversation Starters . 128

CHAPTER 6 – Hospital Admissions: Practice Drills for the End . 135
  A Mixing Bowl of Emotions . 136
  Hospital Admissions as Practice Drills . 137

Hospital Means Respite for You . 138
Exposure to Death . 139
If Your Loved One Shares a Room . 139
Give your Loved one Breaks . 140
Nursing home Conversations . 142
When Your Loved One Wants to Return Home . 143
Bring Humor to the Hospital . 144
Discharge Blues . 145
Practical Tips . 146
Conversation Starters . 150

CHAPTER 7 - The Final Moment Has Come . 155
The Call . 156
Comfort Care Not Life-Extending Care . 158
Looking After Yourself . 159
What if My Loved One Passes When I Leave Their Room? . 159
Communicate Your Love . 160
Acts of Kindness . 161
Final Words . 162
Use Humor to Break the Tension . 164
The Dying Process – What to Expect . 166
My Grandmother's Passing . 168
The Immediate Aftermath of your Loved One's Passing . 171
Back Home from Hospital . 173
Bereavement Services . 174
Conversation Starters . 174

CHAPTER 8 – The Aftermath: Traveling Ahead Without Your Loved One . 179
Early Days and Weeks . 180
The Business Side of Death . 181
The Loss of Your Caregiving Job . 183

Your Loved One's Belongings . 185
Closing the Door . 187
Engage in Activities . 188
Caregiver Post-Traumatic Stress Disorder . 189
Caregiver Guilt . 190
Reminders of Death . 191
A String of Pearls . 192
Reminders of Caregiving . 193
Conversation Starters . 194

Conclusion . 199

A Prayer for the Caregiver . 201

Acknowledgements . 203

Recommended Reading . 207

Index . 209

Permissions and Acknowledgements . 213

About the Author . 217

xii

Introduction

> *There are a thousand ways to kneel*
> *And kiss the ground;*
> *There are a thousand ways*
> *To go home again.*
>
> Rumi

In the scorching summer of 2014, I left behind the Arizona desert and boarded a plane bound for Sydney, Australia where a chilly winter had settled in. Across the globe, both my uncle and grandmother were living with end-stage cancer. My aunt was struggling to manage both of them as each took turns going in and out of hospital. I knew my presence in Australia would help immensely and more importantly, give me an opportunity to say goodbye. My return flight to Phoenix was booked for six weeks later when I assumed both my uncle and grandmother would likely have passed although I was willing to reschedule my flight and stay a few weeks longer if that wasn't the case. I knew dying didn't always fit conveniently into planned schedules.

While on the long, cramped flight across the vast Pacific Ocean, my uncle required emergency surgery to prolong his life. Unfortunately, the word *prolong* doesn't always refer to the best-case scenario. My uncle who loved photography, airplanes, and astronomy died four weeks later aged 66.

As for my grandmother, I arrived at her tiny one-bedroom government housing unit to find her clearly unable to care for herself. She had recently come home from hospital following a blood transfusion. Mildly confused, Nana often forgot her medications and was periodically losing control of her bowels. Dust covered the sweet little knick-knacks she so loved that sat upon small shelves in her living room and the bathroom was a disaster. It was a far cry from the meticulously clean home Nana usually kept.

My aunt hurriedly stopped by my grandmother's unit the day I arrived to explain the dispensing of Nana's daily medications. Until now, a kind neighbor had been trying, with varied degrees of success, to remind my grandmother to take them. Now I was in charge. My jet-lagged brain struggled to comprehend the many medications laid out on the table before me.

I didn't know it at the time but that day marked the beginning of a journey that lasted one and a half years. Living out of my suitcase the entire time, eventually I had to buy additional clothes for seasons I hadn't planned for. So much for my six weeks return flight back to Phoenix! In retrospect, it was probably just as well I didn't know what lay ahead. I may not have believed it anyway. Sometimes a very sick person lives much longer than the experienced predictions of the finest doctors. That was the case with my grandmother. By all appearances, Nana was a physically small and frail woman who might blow over from the slightest puff of wind. Yet despite her size and terminal cancer, she was made of tough stuff.

My grandmother and I had always been close. When she continued living beyond medical estimates rather than quickly succumbing to her disease, I knew couldn't leave her and return to Phoenix. Nana had done so much for me over the course of my life and this was an opportunity to give something back to her. Becoming her sole caregiver was an unplanned life-changing experience.

It's my intention in writing this book, that the journey my grandmother and I took together will benefit you, as you care for your terminally ill loved one. Perhaps like me, you have never been a caregiver before and are feeling completely overwhelmed. Perhaps you're wondering whether you'll be able to handle the many unknowns that lie ahead. I hope my experiences as an unprepared, learn-on-the-job caregiver increase your awareness of the caregiving role, strengthen the relationship between you and your loved one, and fortify your courage for the days ahead.

Love, Laughter, and Morphine is divided into eight chapters with poems and quotes scattered among the pages like seeds in a garden. Conversation Starters, designed to provide suggestions for meaningful discourse between you, your loved one, and significant others are included at the end of most chapters as well as numerous Practical Tips. Certain subjects, such as caregiver stress and relationship concerns are by necessity discussed in a variety of forms among several chapters.

Chapter 1, *First Steps on a Long Road*, provides an overview of the caregiving journey including ways to organize the business side of illness, decrease stress, and build a relationship with your loved one based upon mutual understanding.

Chapter 2, *You the Caregiver: No Batteries, Love Powered*, discusses *you*, a special person who has taken on a rewarding but challenging job. The emotional and physical impacts of caregiving are examined including the importance of caring for yourself.

In Chapter 3, *The One You Are Caring For*, the discussion turns towards your terminally ill loved one. How is he or she feeling emotionally, physically, and spiritually? What insights can be gleaned by looking at illness through their eyes? How can we as caregivers develop greater compassion, patience, and understanding? These questions are addressed in this chapter.

Chapter 4, *Family and Friends*, examines the supportive role friends and family members play in caregiving. Nipping potential problems in the bud are also covered.

Chapter 5, *The Palliative Care Team and Other Supporters*, sheds light upon the roles of these essential professionals. This chapter emphasizes the value of listening to experienced recommendations, asking questions, and forging good working relationships. You may even choose to refer to this chapter early to familiarize yourself with members of the team.

Chapter 6, *Hospital Admissions: Practice Drills for the End*, covers the expectations and preparation for in-patient admissions. Suggestions for breaking up your loved one's long days as a patient are also included.

Chapter 7, *The Final Moment Has Come*, concerns the passing of your dear loved one and the end of your caregiving journey together. Common expectations as death arrives and the need to comfort yourself during this sorrowful time are gently examined.

Chapter 8, *Life After Caregiving: Traveling Ahead Without Your Loved One*, concerns heart-breaking grief, the business side of death, and the loss of your caregiving role. Caregiver PTSD and guilt are addressed as well as ways to heal and slowly move forward.

An inconvenience is
an adventure wrongly considered.

C.K. Chesterton

It is my sincere hope that *Love, Laughter, and Morphine* becomes a familiar companion on your brave journey; offering comfort, encouragement, and helpful suggestions along the way. You may even enjoy a laugh or two as you discover the amusing side of caregiving and yes, there is one. More importantly, please remember that you are never alone although you may feel that way at times. There are many of us who have walked the caregiving path or are current caregivers. May you can feel our collective presence and support as you care for your loved one and walk him or her Home.

Chapter 1

First Steps on a Long Road

*We are all in the same boat
In a stormy sea
And we owe each other
A terrible loyalty.*

C.K. Chesterton

Climbing into the back seat of the taxi that cold July morning, I didn't know whether the sky was cloudy or clear. My mind was elsewhere. The drive from Sydney's Kingsford-Smith International Airport to my grandmother's small, one-bedroom government housing unit in the suburbs was a blur. While flying from Los Angeles, my uncle had undergone emergency surgery due to colon cancer complications. I didn't know as yet whether he had survived the operation. Meanwhile, my 94-year-old grandmother had end-stage colorectal cancer and was not expected to live beyond a few months at most. She'd been discharged from hospital only one week earlier following a blood transfusion. My family and I often wondered who would pass away first – Uncle Terry or Nana? We expected both of them to be gone by Christmas.

My six weeks visit to Australia was a way of helping my family but more importantly, it was an opportunity to say goodbye. Uncle Terry survived his surgery, waking up with an unwanted colostomy bag attached to his abdomen. Sadly, he only lived another four weeks. My grandmother however, went on to live another 14 months – far beyond the estimates of experienced doctors. While my aunt grieved her husband's passing and faced the impending loss of her mother, I became Nana's sole caregiver. Landing at the airport that winter morning, I couldn't imagine how events were going to play themselves out. Without knowing it, I was in for a quite an experience; an adventure of the heart!

My family and I were very close to my grandmother. She was our beloved matriarch; the keeper of family stories and memories and she wasn't going to get better. But in her 90's, Nana was fortunate to be at the end of a long life unlike Uncle Terry for whom cancer had other plans. As Nana's caregiver I was walking her Home on a path that was new for both of us. Immediately overwhelmed by the many unknowns, I didn't know where to begin. You may be feeling the same way now in regards to caring for your loved one.

A Brief Overview of Caregiving

Caregiving is an offering, a practice of giving care to another. Caregiving requires a donation of body, mind, and spirit; that donation will come from you. Like me, you won't know with any certainty how long it will take you and your loved one to traverse *the valley of the shadow of death.* The journey might take days, weeks, months, or years. Feeling a garden full of butterflies flapping their wings inside your stomach is normal. It means you're ready to learn, grow, and like all of us, make mistakes. It's no small thing to take that first shaky step as a caregiver but take it anyway. You are braver and stronger than you know.

Being a caregiver also means bearing unique responsibilities many of which are heavy. The one you care for is gradually succumbing to his or her illness and part of how he or she experiences their final days, weeks, or months rests with you. You'll sacrifice much time and effort. Your life will no longer be what it once was and you will no longer be who you once were. Your world will now intertwine with that of your loved one. In many ways you'll become inseparable like twisted, tangled vines growing upon an ancient tree in a rainforest.

Despite the fact that each caregiver and situation is unique, caregivers typically share much in common. The foremost is the presence of stress. You'll need to acquire skills that minimize, as much as possible, the pressure of performing endless tasks while tired and filled with anticipatory grief. Sleep-deprivation, frustration, and loneliness also appear but thankfully, there'll be many moments of love, humor, and compassion. Caregiving can be a deeply rewarding and meaningful experience despite the inherent difficulties of caring for someone so unwell.

It's important to note that not everyone chooses or wants to be a caregiver. While I was happy to remain in Australia as my grandmother's caregiver (despite not knowing what that entailed), there are some men, women, and even children who become reluctant caregivers when there are no other options available. Not wanting to provide care for whatever reason, makes the journey far more difficult. Instead of a meaningful desire to walk your loved one Home, you may feel as though you're being dragged; kicking and screaming the entire way! If there's no other choice outside of having to provide care, remind yourself that the only thing you *do* have control over are your thoughts. Use your thoughts, your attitude, to turn a rough road into one that's less harsh. Life can be unfair at times but don't believe in a bottomless pit. Plunge into the deep, dark well of your anger and fear. Touch the bottom of the muck and mire, then slowly resurface and transform these powerful emotions into something healthier and more meaningful. Grow. It's a tall order. Much easier said than done but don't simply survive caregiving. Ask for help but please don't wake up each morning and spit at life. You deserve better than that and so does your loved one.

It's Normal to Feel Overwhelmed and Upset

Neither you nor your loved one asked for a terminal illness to turn your lives upside down but here you both are. It's normal to feel upset, to experience grief in the face of impending loss; the loss of what was once familiar and known. Be prepared for the many emotions that will arise as you embark upon this caregiving journey - sadness, anger, fear, guilt, frustration, and anxiety. Give yourself permission to feel them while wondering what lies ahead and how you can possibly manage it all.

It is not uncommon for caregivers to also experience depression. This must be addressed and prioritized if it arises. Depression is more than simply feeling down or a little blue. Depression is a serious mental health condition. Don't try to manage despair on your own. Let your loved one's palliative care team and your own doctor know if you're suffering. Don't tell yourself that you're too busy to attend to depression and attempt to soldier through it. That never works. If you don't look after yourself, you won't be able to look after your loved one. It's as simple as that. More importantly, you don't deserve to suffer. We all have mental health challenges at times, even when we aren't caregiving but caregiving puts much more pressure upon us. Remember, you're not Wonder Woman or Superman even if you do look good in spandex! Taking care of your own needs is imperative and in the case of depression, non-negotiable.

Feeling overwhelmed by the responsibility of having so much of your loved one's life within your hands is normal. Personally, I often felt that the weight of caring for my grandmother was going to crush me. I had enough love for the job but worried I wasn't strong in other ways. Often, I was afraid of the great unknown. How would I cope with my grandmother's passing and *when* would the end come?

Anticipatory grief over your loved one's inevitable passing will climb upon your back like a gorilla, holding on with a vice-like grip. Some days, this grief will feel quite cumbersome. Find a trusted family member or friend to talk to about your sorrow. It's heart-wrenching watching your loved one deteriorate before your eyes. Don't attempt to keep this sadness inside you. It's too large. Share it.

Life is brief
But love is LONG.

Alfred Lord Tennyson

Be Ready to Make Mistakes

In the face of terminal illness, it's normal to feel wildly beyond your comfort zone. Unless you're a professionally trained caregiver or person with prior experience, you'll learn on the job just as I did. Accept the fact that you'll mess up occasionally. Making mistakes is almost a prerequisite for becoming a better caregiver.

Preparation for Caregiving

The best time to lay the groundwork for caregiving is now. Organization and the implementation of good habits from the onset is crucial. Don't wait until you become exhausted before trying to do things differently. If something isn't working well from the beginning, it will likely get worse. Expect a variety of changes along the caregiving path and prepare for them by standing firm upon a sensible, working foundation. If you or your family can afford full or part-time in-home nursing care, medical equipment, housekeeping or other additional caregiving assistance, consider yourself very fortunate. Those services will help you immensely. But for those of you with limited resources such as I had, please utilize at least some of the recommendations laid out in this book.

For instance, buy a few notebooks as well as envelopes or folders of different sizes and use them to keep track of all the many bits 'n pieces that caring for your loved one will involve. You'll be surprised at the many and varied items you'll need to keep track of. Medications are an important example. Over the course of your loved one's illness, he or she will require numerous medications to manage symptoms. Along the way, doctors will add new drugs, remove others, change the dosage or switch from tablet form to liquid, quicker than Winnie the Pooh can eat a jar of honey! Keeping up with these frequent changes can keep you busy. Being organized helps ensure your loved one will always have available the medications he or she needs, *when* he or she needs them. More about medication at the end of this chapter.

In addition, there'll be increasing amounts of paperwork, receipts, and phone numbers as well as educational booklets. You'll need to know where you can find specific information when you need to access it quickly.

Consider this adventure metaphor: none of us would attempt to summit Mt. Everest without being prepared. Careful thought and planning are necessary for any arduous climb. We'd acquire the proper equipment, warm clothing, and hire experienced Sherpas to guide us. Without this foundation, we'd be inviting disaster. Likewise, in caregiving, being as prepared as possible given the variables, will make a huge difference to your ability to provide care for your loved one and minimize stress. Professional mountain climbers know that successfully summiting any peak requires mental and physical readiness. Caregiving is also a rough trek with many twists, turns, and blind corners – it will be your Mt. Everest. Knowing what to expect and laying the groundwork early on will make your expedition into the unknown far more manageable. Don't wait for the cow manure to hit the fan before straightening up the business side of caregiving!

Sleep Deprivation

As your loved one deteriorates, he or she will increasingly need your assistance during the night. Toileting, dispensing medication for breakthrough pain, and repositioning in bed to prevent bedsores are tasks that will require your weary body once the sun sets. Aside from directly helping your loved one with their needs, you'll likely find yourself lying awake at night worrying about him or her. You'll listen for the sounds of their breathing and find yourself frequently getting up and checking on them.

On-duty around the clock, broken sleep can easily become a continuous state of sleep-deprivation for caregivers. Lack of quality sleep can negatively impact your mental and physical health. You may find that your ability to think clearly and make wise decisions falls by the wayside. During this time, it's especially important to seek help and input from the professionals around you. Sleep-deprivation isn't something you can work through and learn to tolerate long term. You'll fall flat on your face and who will care for your loved one when that happens? Please ask for help.

Monitor Your Loved One

As your loved one's caregiver, you are the person aside from doctors and nurses, who'll likely notice changes in their physical and mental condition. You're the person deciding when to contact members of the palliative care team, hospital, or other community services. Although the palliative care team will work closely by your side, no-one else will spend as much time with your loved one other than you. While at home alone with him or her, you're in charge. The realization of this fact can be quite daunting when it hits you.

If at any time you're unsure of a particular change in your loved one's condition or feel hesitant to carry out the responsibility of caregiving, contact the palliative care team. They're readily available to assist you.

Take Breaks While You Can

There are many ways in which your situation will change as your loved one's illness progresses. At varying rates of speed ranging from a snail's pace to a rattlesnake strike, caregiving can morph into something requiring more of your time, effort, and emotions. *Now* may be the prime opportunity for you to take breaks. It's probable that your loved one is currently at their highest level of mental and physical functioning. With passing time, his or her needs and dependence upon you will increase. Although you may feel tired and stressed at the present moment, you might not realize how much more tired and stressed you will become. That was certainly true of me when I began caregiving. I couldn't conceive of what *worse* would look and feel like.

It's important to keep in mind that not knowing how much time your loved one has remaining, may result in a reluctance to take breaks away from him or her. Speaking for myself, I was definitely afraid to leave my grandmother or travel too far away from her home. Also, as caregivers, we want to spend as much time as we can with those we love. While doctors can provide us with an approximate time-frame for our loved one's passing, we know life doesn't always play out as planned or expected – not for doctors, not for caregivers. A loved one may pass away much sooner or later than the best educated prediction. In the beginning of my caregiving experience, I would have taken more breaks had I known how long Nana was going to live. Unfortunately, doctors don't have crystal balls and some patients, like my grandmother, don't follow the norm. For better or worse, we can only make decisions based upon what is known or predicted at the time. Community nurses and the palliative care team encouraged me to take breaks and go out for a few hours but I felt such a responsibility to my grandmother that I couldn't imagine 'abandoning' her. What if something were to happen? What if she took a fall? What if she had some kind of medical event or emergency while I was away? That worry kept me with her. You too may find yourself in the same boat regarding breaks. But do keep in mind that your loved one may possibly be at their best now and moments of respite may be easier to take at this time.

Relationship Issues

All relationships, even close ones, are put to the test during any terminal illness. But strong relationships endure and navigate rough seas far better than poor relationships do. Taking the time to understand how you and your loved one are personally affected by the illness is important. You had a relationship prior to the diagnosis. It may have been healthy and warm-hearted or it may have been strained. Unfortunately, the stress of accepting and managing a terminal illness may add fuel to the fire if neither of you ever got along. The onus of improving the relationship however, lies heavier for you as the caregiver. To be lovingly blunt, you aren't the person deteriorating and knowingly losing their life in the near future. By necessity, by compassion, you may need to be the bigger person in this relationship. Fortunately, it's never too late to forgive, make peace, and begin again. It's never too late to arrive at a mutual understanding and nurture a small seedling of love and respect for one another. It benefits both of you to find common ground.

Although you and the one you're caring for are walking this final path together, each of you will experience it differently. Gathering insight into one another's feelings will help you grow closer. The roles you had prior to the illness will change during caregiving. Do you have the courage to initiate heart-felt conversations going forward into this new territory? Later chapters will discuss this in more detail.

Fortunately, my grandmother and I had a close relationship prior to her illness. This helped immensely as we endured endless ups and downs. This is not to say caring for Nana was smooth sailing. It wasn't. It's not to say we didn't get upset or impatient with one another. We did. It isn't to say we always understood where the other was coming from. We didn't. As an example, at the end of a long day, Nana might ask me for one small thing and suddenly it became one request too many. As I replied, "Just a minute," my voice had a tone to it. Overwhelmed, I simply needed to sit and rest for five minutes, perhaps enjoy a cup of hot tea in peace without interruption. At times, I felt my grandmother didn't understand how tired I was or notice that I was never resting. From Nana's standpoint however, she was too sick to do even small things for herself and probably hated to ask for help but didn't have a choice. We both worked on becoming more understanding. A swinging pendulum of emotions is normal for everyone but good relationships minimize those unpleasant moments.

Encourage Open Communication

Honest communication between yourself and your loved one is important for the path ahead and a vital component of any healthy relationship. It's true that some individuals are naturally more open to sharing their concerns and feelings, while others are shy or private. Caring for someone who keeps their feelings to themselves however, makes it challenging to know how they are doing each day and how best to assist them.

Despite your best efforts, your loved one may not be forthcoming with information you might need to know as their caregiver. He or she may also communicate with you differently than with someone else. My grandmother for example, often told community nurses that she was fine even though ten minutes earlier she may have told me she was feeling nauseous or in pain. Once, I corrected her in front of a nurse (something I soon learned to do privately) and Nana responded, "My granddaughter exaggerates!" I was taken aback by her comment but thought quick enough to ask Nana why her nose was growing as long as Pinocchio's! Don't be surprised if your loved one seems to rally when community nurses or members of the palliative care team are visiting in your home.

Active listening is a powerful element of good communication. Hear what your loved one is really saying. At times, he or she may speak in a round-about way before feeling comfortable enough to articulate what's truly on his or her mind. In addition, listen not only to what your loved one says but also to what is left unsaid. In particular, learn to become a reader of body language by listening with your eyes as well as your ears. There were many times for example, when Nana didn't mention to me directly that she was in pain but I noticed her grimacing when she tried to stand, sit, or shift position upon a chair or in bed. When I asked if she was hurting, she softly replied, "It's nothing I can't handle. There are other people worse off." Of course, pain and discomfort aren't something your loved one should have to 'handle.' I believe at least some of my grandmother's reluctance to mention pain before I asked her about it was probably generational and perhaps cultural as well. She was a Great Depression and WWII-era Aussie raised not to complain. Later, as her cancer progressed and pain increased, she did verbally ask for pain medication. This alerted me to the fact that her pain level was undoubtedly intense.

The Nursing Home Discussion

Placing a loved one into the care of a nursing home is a terribly sad thing for most of us to contemplate. Whether a nursing home admission is planned for the final stages of your loved one's illness or a place to avoid, discussing all options is important. Despite abusive situations that occasionally make news headlines, many nursing facilities are caring and professional. There are benefits to nursing homes in certain circumstances especially when other options are few.

Social workers will likely broach this subject first. These professionals want to hear your thoughts and concerns regarding possible placement. Be honest with them. Is it your goal to keep your loved one out of a nursing home entirely? Are you wanting your loved one to remain at home for as long as possible and then choose a nursing facility? Social workers are well-versed in the many issues surrounding this topic. Allow them to smooth the rough edges of this difficult and heartbreaking decision. Certainly, there's no harm in gathering information and discussing this possibility should your loved one require more extensive care than you can provide. Awareness of this option serves to strengthen your caregiving safety net should you need it.

My grandmother didn't want to enter a nursing home. She was adamant about it and often cried whenever the possibility was mentioned. Being emotionally close to this small, frail woman, I felt it was entirely up to me to protect the integrity of her final wish and keep her out of one. Without Nana realizing it however, her request to remain at home placed quite a burden upon me. Towards the very end of her life, I was on the emotional and physical brink of what I had left to give. My health was becoming affected. The palliative care team gently nudged and spelled it out for me, yet I kept hoping for some kind of miracle – one that would give me super-human powers to keep my grandmother home. Instead, I remained a mere mortal and struggled terribly with the nursing home option. I felt I'd be a caregiving failure if a nursing facility was chosen; that I would let my grandmother down. As her caregiver, I pushed myself hard. Looking back now, had Nana told me she'd be willing to enter a nursing home if necessary, her acceptance would have eased my anguish in feeling I had failed her.

Work through the unpleasant emotions that often accompany this sad subject. Speak with your social worker and the one you're caring for. Initiating a discussion may be as simple as asking your loved one, "If there comes a time when I'm no longer able to care for you as well as I would like and as well as you deserve, would you be willing to enter a nursing home where I can come and visit you as often as possible?" Be brave and discuss this sensitive topic ahead of time. Don't wait until circumstances force you to make a decision. That's far too stressful.

> *The world is not divided*
> *Into the strong who care*
> *And the weak who are cared for.*
> *We must each in turn care and be cared for,*
> *Not just because it is good for us,*
> *But because it is the way things are.*
>
> Sheila Cassidy

Accept and Seek Assistance

If you're an inexperienced caregiver, listen to those around you who do have experience. Professionals such as doctors, nurses, social workers, and pastoral care will be your primary sources of information and support. These individuals have built their careers around caring for those with serious and terminal illnesses. Please heed their advice and guidance. They are able to look at your caregiving situation objectively when you cannot. In addition, they have access to a variety of community and government resources which may be helpful to you. Fears grow when questions aren't asked and concerns aren't verbalized. Please don't allow yourself to worry needlessly. Accept and ask for help.

Share the Care

At times, our loved one might be reluctant to allow anyone other than us to assist in their care. Clearly, this can evolve into an unhealthy situation. An example of this was the first time a volunteer community caregiver sat with my grandmother while I went to a doctor's appointment. Nana told me she felt capable of looking after herself while I was away and didn't want a *stranger* to sit with her. Although I hated to upset Nana, I didn't feel comfortable leaving her alone. She had already fallen once in the kitchen and I didn't want that to happen again. Arriving back home following my appointment, I was delighted to hear that Nana really enjoyed chatting with the volunteer and wouldn't mind if she came again someday! Initially, Nana was reluctant for me to leave her with someone else but in the end, it was a baby step that worked out well for both of us.

Spiritual Considerations

For some individuals, terminal illness results in a deepening of their faith while others may stumble with doubts. Everyone is different in how the disease and prospect of impending death affects them. Experiencing the ups and downs of illness either as the patient or the caregiver can easily rattle one's heart and mind. Should you experience spiritual concerns and desire comforting guidance, seek out a representative of your particular faith. You can also speak with palliative care staff such as chaplains or pastoral care.

For those of you with no specific spiritual or religious beliefs, questions and concerns regarding the finality of death still arise and may cause anxiety. Pastoral care can also address this profound unease without introducing religion. The mission of palliative care is to alleviate, where possible, suffering in all its many forms. It matters not whether you're agnostic, Presbyterian, Buddhist, or an atheist. Don't suffer silently in constant fear of what tomorrow might bring. Let others support you upon your journey as you endeavor to make peace with the inevitable. These are difficult days. Reach out and communicate your distress. Help is available. Grab it and hold on.

Maintain a Routine for Your Loved One

Psychologically it's important for your loved one to maintain as much of their daily routine as possible. Routine signifies familiarity and comfort. With all the changes that are taking place inside his or her weakening body and with life's great mystery looming ahead, adhering at least loosely to usual customs greatly supports his or her mental health. Eventually, much will change and new routines of caregiving will create a different framework. Holding on to as many habitual activities as you can, while you're able, provides solace for your loved one.

Mindfulness

Being mindful of the present moment in which you breathe is a wonderful practice for caregivers. In a nutshell, mindfulness refers to gently keeping your mind, that is, your non-judgmental awareness, where your body is. Mindfulness is derived from Eastern meditation practices and can assist you in lowering stress, feeling more centered, and calm. Practicing mindfulness can also improve physical well-being as the tension we so often store in our tight muscles is released.

For example, while washing dishes, wash them with awareness as opposed to anxiously wondering what tomorrow will bring. Feel the warm water and tingle of soap suds upon your skin. Feel the shape and texture of the plates and bowls you're cleaning. While feeding dinner to your loved one, be aware of how beautiful his or her face is and the aroma of the food being served.

Present moment awareness can ameliorate the overwhelming fatigue and stress that typically envelop caregivers. Mindfulness is not refusing to accept what has occurred nor the avoidance of what is to come, but rather living in the only moment you can reasonably handle – the present. The benefits of mindfulness are well documented. There are many wonderful books available on the subject of mindfulness as well as classes that teach it. Although free time is at a premium for you as a caregiver, do what you can to learn more about this valuable practice.

Watch your way then, as a cautious traveler;
And don't be gazing at that mountain
Or river in the distance, and saying,
"How shall I get over them?"
But keep to the present little inch
That is before you,
And accomplish that in the little moment
That belongs to it.
The mountain and the river can only
Be passed in the same way; and,
When you come to them,
You will come to the light and strength
That belong to them.

M.A. Kelty

Use Humor

A sense of humor can go a long way toward easing the tension of difficult circumstances. It may seem strange that humor could ever have a place in caring for a terminally ill loved one but it can. The emotional rejuvenation that results will feel good for both of you. There is something normalizing about humor. Laughter brings perspective to situations in which we have little control. Levity can lift some of the dark clouds that surround being unwell.

One example involved a composition book in which I kept daily medical notes. Diligently, I'd write Nana's response to changes in her medication, whether or not she had a bowel movement, her level of pain and nausea, amount of rectal bleeding, and level of confusion as well as anything out of the ordinary. This information was useful for doctors and community nurses to recognize patterns and trends as Nana's colorectal cancer progressed. My grandmother was aware of my notetaking and often wondered how I could find so much to write about. I used to refer to the journal as her 'Bum Book.'

This always made her laugh. I often teased Nana by telling her I was going to publish it when she passed away and that her Bum Book was sure to become a best seller! Strange, but perhaps in some small way this book you're now reading is indeed Nana's Bum Book. I wonder what she would think of it?

Practical Tips

1. Dealing with Medications

Organizing your loved one's medications is one of the most important things to do early upon your caregiving adventure. Quite likely, the number of medications he or she is taking will increase over time. Towards the end of my grandmother's life she was taking 15 different medications, all of them running out at varying times. Without a workable, organized system of management it would have been impossible for me to keep track of them all.

Be aware that certain medications especially controlled substances such as opioids, require strict monitoring by your loved one's doctor and you will not be given automatic refills. Keep your loved one as pain-free as possible by not allowing medications to completely run out prior to refilling them. Familiarize yourself with all refill policies.

Also keep in mind that your loved one's medications may possibly come from more than one doctor or facility. Nana received medications through her General Practitioner, a community service known as Nurses on Wheels (in contact with her GP), and the doctor at the palliative care hospital where she was a patient. Initially this confused me as I didn't know which medications were from which doctor or facility and I didn't know who to contact to receive additional prescriptions. Nana had tablets, capsules, patches, liquids, pre-filled syringes, gels, and sprays! At one point, there was a compounding laboratory in the mix. I was bewildered, not knowing who was ultimately in charge. Later, I learned that what appeared chaotic to me, involved organized communication between Nana's GP, Nurses on Wheels, and her doctor at the palliative care hospital.

As I first began caring for my grandmother, I was jet-lagged and overwhelmed. There were countless tasks before me. On top of that, the knowledge that this tiny, much-loved woman was going to die, filled me with sorrow. Even though Nana had lived a long life, I felt utterly heart-broken and selfishly wished she could live forever. Not thinking clearly, I was refilling her medications one at a time. Yes, one at a time! As you can imagine, chasing after medications occupied much of my time. I didn't have a car and needed to rely upon either my tired legs or public transportation in order to visit the doctor or pharmacist on Nana's behalf. Thankfully, during one of Nana's hospitalizations, I was able to rest and de-stress. Finally, it dawned on me to group her medications together according to when they were close to running out. When I began doing that, it made all the difference in the world! I refilled several meds at a time instead of one at a time. Managing Nana's wheelbarrow load of medications became far less stressful and saved me many trips in inclement weather. I couldn't believe I didn't think of it before! This is what happens when 'caregiver's brain' takes over – formerly functioning grey matter is replaced by the brain of a garden slug!

Do yourself a favor, make a list of each medication and write down the exact date they run out. Then review those dates and group medications together according to those that will run out close to the same time – say, within a week or so of one another. Then refill those meds at the same time. You can thank me later!

Also, if you take prescription medications for yourself, you may want to consider grouping your own medications on the bottom of your loved one's list to save time and unnecessary trips on your own behalf. As a caregiver, it's easy to let yourself fall through the cracks.

An important item to purchase is a large plastic pill dispenser. My grandmother took her medications at four different times during the day as well as additional meds for break-through pain or nausea. I bought a dispenser that included all of the time periods I needed. Although the container could hold one weeks' worth of medication, I never put more than a few days' worth of pills in it. I didn't want Nana helping herself to medication without me knowing it especially if she was confused. Coming out of the bathroom one afternoon, I caught her searching for pain medication. My grandmother didn't know which tablets were for pain or how many to take. For safety's sake, I kept the main supply of medications (enough to knock out a woolly mammoth) up high in a cupboard where she couldn't reach them. Also, with Nana's medications and dosages changing so frequently it made sense to only fill the dispenser for a few days at a time.

In addition, keep an updated list of your loved one's medications including dosage, how often they're dispensed, and any known allergies in a convenient location. The palliative care team and community nurses will frequently ask you for this information to ensure that everyone is on the same page.

2. *Keep Track of Important Information and Phone Numbers*

Buy a small notebook and/or business card holder for important contact information and keep it in a handy location. Write phone numbers, addresses, and emails of your loved one's doctors, hospital front desk, members of the palliative care team, community nurses, health insurance company or government agencies, pharmacist, and other community services.

In addition, use a large envelope or file folder to keep important papers such as medical and pharmaceutical receipts, records, and legal documents such as Advanced Directives and Do Not Resuscitate orders. Later on, you'll appreciate having done this.

3. Keep Track of Your Loved One's Daily Medical Condition

Keep a notebook (remember the Bum Book?) in which to record information regarding your loved one's daily medical condition. Are there any patterns or trends you notice? Rate your loved one's pain level from zero to ten as well as nausea and activity level. Does your loved one alternate between feeling hot and cold? Is he or she coughing? What is his or her appetite like? Is your loved one sleeping more each day? Have you noticed any bedsores? Did he or she have a bowel movement and did it look normal? Is your loved one experiencing any mental confusion? Doctors and community nurses will appreciate this information.

4. Medical Equipment and Aids

Be aware that your loved one will require more assistive medical equipment as he or she gradually loses functionality and mobility. Devices may come in the form of canes, walkers, wheelchairs, toilet raisers, donut cushions, bed rails, special mattresses, slide sheets, and bathroom safety equipment. There are countless pieces of equipment available that can make daily life for your loved one and yourself much easier.

Find out who you need to contact in order to rent or buy medical equipment. Occupational Therapists (OTs) operating through your loved one's hospital can assist you in their proper and safe use. Have their contact information available. Usually the hospital or independent medical supply companies can deliver equipment to your home especially if it's bulky or heavy. Ask if they give discounts for multiple equipment rentals.

Also, buy a bedside bell for your loved one so that he or she can ring it when they need you. A bell is especially handy at night if you're sleeping or working in a separate room from your loved one. Make sure the bell is kept in a location that's easy for your loved one to reach without knocking it over or hurting themselves.

5. Safety Concerns

You will need to create safe spaces for your loved one especially as their illness progresses and they become weaker. Occupational therapists can help you in regards to safety issues specific to your home. Here are a few general examples:

- Remove rugs and mats that easily slide.
- Re-route any electrical cords that your loved one may trip on
- Take note of any furniture legs that stick out and might be a tripping hazard.
- Make sure you have slip-resistant mats in the bathroom.
- Install a safety bar in the shower or bathtub.
- Purchase a shower chair or slide-across bath bench.
- Be mindful of door snakes (that prevent cold drafts) as they can become a tripping hazard when going in and out of doorways.
- Be aware of any steps or raised areas inside or outside the home.
- Make sure your loved one doesn't have to stretch or attempt to climb up on a stool in order to reach an object they frequently use.

Aside from your loved one's physical limitations, an important factor affecting safety is his or her cognitive abilities. Does your loved one become confused at times? When I first arrived at my grandmother's home, I noticed she often turned on wrong switches when using the stovetop and oven. Occasionally, she left an oven mitt or tea towel on top of a hot stove. I was a nervous wreck waiting for the house to burn down! Fortunately, that never happened but I took over the cooking early on in large part because of my concerns. Be alert to any confusion your loved one shows that may affect their safety and yours. More about cognitive issues in a later chapter.

6. *Disposable Underwear and Bathroom Issues*

Loss of bladder and bowel control may occur as muscles weaken. Be prepared for your loved one to experience these issues by having a few items such as disposable underwear, baby wipes, and cleaning products available *before* accidents happen. This aspect of their illness will challenge both of you. Be sensitive and compassionate in regards to the embarrassment your loved one feels following an accident. He or she is too unwell to clean up their own mess and this upsets them. Our beautiful loved ones can easily feel they're a bother to us when this happens.

Initially, my grandmother wasn't wearing disposable undergarments. I was constantly washing soiled underwear, slacks, socks, nightgowns, and bedsheets. As Nana had no clothes dryer in her tiny housing unit, I could only hang her clothes to dry on the outside clothesline. Washing and drying quickly became a problem for me during days or weeks of rain as well as during winter months. Blood, mucous, and loose stools were an unfortunate and inevitable occurrence with my grandmother's colorectal cancer. For several months following my arrival, she was resistant to wearing disposable underwear. Her cognition wasn't good at that time and she didn't realize how difficult it was for me to stay on top of keeping her clothes clean. Often, Nana didn't know how bad a particular accident was as I tried to shield her from the knowledge of it and protect her dignity as much as I could. She may also have viewed disposable underwear as symbolic of a loss of independence; perhaps a reversion back to childhood.

One morning I was feeling optimistic about persuading Nana to change her mind about the disposable underwear. I propositioned her to wear a pair of them for one hour and then tell me what she thought of them. If she really didn't like them when the hour was up, I'd no longer mention wearing them to her. Using my wits (aka stealth and deception), I deliberately turned on an enthralling television program for her to watch. At the end of the hour I asked her how the underwear felt. Nana replied, "Oh, I forgot I was even wearing them!" I was beaming from ear to ear! She wore disposable underwear from that day onward. Yay, for the caregiver! I felt smug for the rest of the day!

Make sure you have plenty of disposable underwear on hand once your loved one begins wearing them. You'll go through them rather quickly. Also keep extra toilet paper on hand as incontinence issues mean more wiping. Baby wipes are also a good addition for your loved one's sensitive skin. There are many types of baby wipes available. Some are advertised as flushable but make sure that's printed on the package before discarding them into the toilet bowl otherwise, you'll end up needing a plumber!

Unfortunately, as Nana's illness progressed, she lost weight and the 'Size Small' disposable underwear she wore was no longer snug enough to form a seal around her upper legs and torso. There was leakage at the top of her legs and when she reclined in bed there was leakage along her back via the loose waistband. A helpful community nurse gave me several waterproof pads called Chux bed pads to place beneath Nana at night to protect the bed sheets and mattress. These rectangular pads can be purchased at the pharmacy, medical supply companies, and online. Chux are also useful to place on top of your loved one's favorite chair to protect cushions from leaks. Be sure to keep some on hand.

In the bathroom, place items you may need to reach quickly in a close and convenient location. At a discount store I bought a small plastic table with shelves and placed it beside the toilet where I could easily grab what I needed. On the shelves I kept a box of latex gloves, baby wipes, anti-bacterial wipes for cleaning the toilet seat, a stack of disposable undergarments, feminine hygiene pads for rectal bleeds, a box of scented garbage bin liners, and extra rolls of toilet paper.

Organizing the bathroom and being prepared for incontinence issues ahead of time will help you enormously. Being ready to address accidents quickly protects your loved one from experiencing deeper distress and embarrassment.

7. *Food and Drink*

As your loved one's body changes, their appetite and tolerance for certain foods change. He or she may become fussy even in regards to food they once enjoyed. Feeding your loved one will become one of the most challenging tasks for you as their caregiver. Write down ideas for meals and snacks and ask others to help with suggestions for your picky eater! Eventually, as your loved one nears the time of their passing, he or she will eat and drink far less. I felt sad when I noticed this with my grandmother.

Beverages or food containing ginger are handy for nausea. My grandmother constantly drank ginger beer in small sips throughout the day (for non-Australian readers, ginger beer is non-alcoholic). Ginger ale and crystalized ginger pieces also help some patients. Consult doctors and nurses regarding nausea issues.

At some point on your caregiving journey, you may notice your loved one begin to cough or choke while eating and drinking. This can occur as swallowing muscles weaken. Eventually, you'll need to cut your loved one's food into smaller pieces and provide a bendable straw for drinking. Monitor your loved one while they eat or drink if choking is an issue. Avoid giving him or her anything chewy. Pureed meals will typically be given towards the end of life as these are easier to swallow. Always mention coughing and choking episodes to medical staff as soon as you notice them.

Grocery deliveries are wonderful if they're available in your area especially if you don't have a car. This option became available in my grandmother's community when her condition deteriorated significantly and I could no longer leave her alone. Perfect timing! Thank goodness I'd previously purchased a small computer tablet for Nana to play games on and I was able to order everything we needed online.

Another thing to consider, is the bad aftertaste that certain medications leave, especially those in liquid form. Nana ate a small piece of candy whenever she swallowed these unsavory medicines. She had a sweet tooth and candy was a positive reward for taking medication she'd otherwise baulk at. Once, after handing Nana a piece of candy, I channeled my inner Mary Poppins and sang, "A spoon full of sugar helps the medicine go down." My grandmother almost choked on the candy from laughing and advised me not quit my day job! Candy, tea biscuits, and dry crackers are all useful to have in the pantry should your loved one require something to take away a lingering bad taste.

8. Advanced Directives and Legal Considerations

Many legal issues will arise while caregiving. You may need to make decisions regarding your loved one's finances as well as his or her medical care. Be prepared for these legal issues ahead of time. I wasn't aware that I'd have problems operating on my grandmother's behalf until it came up. Getting permission from Nana and into the hands of those requiring it was challenging especially as she became increasingly unwell. Most of this involved Nana's signature on paperwork but one gentleman wanted Nana's verbal consent over the telephone at a time when her vocal muscles were so weak that she could barely whisper! I had innocently assumed permission wasn't necessary when making decisions on behalf of my dying grandmother. I thought I was free to do willy-nilly as long as it was in her best interests. Obviously, that wasn't the case. Although most of us would genuinely do the right thing on our loved one's behalf, not everyone does. Acquiring legal permission protects our individual rights particularly when we're vulnerable and that's a good thing.

Find out what legal documents are necessary in the state in which your loved one resides. Either you or another family member must have legal permission to not only make medical decisions but also arrangements involving banking, utilities, housing, and so forth on your loved one's behalf. Filling out forms is a nuisance but please don't wait until your loved one has worsened before doing so.

Equally important, find out whether or not your loved one wants life-saving procedures initiated should his or her breathing/cardiac functions become arrested and cease. This would involve such measures as CPR and defibrillation for example. Respect your loved one's wishes even if they differ from your own. You may want them to live as long as possible and take every life-saving measure but letting them go may be the kindest thing to do for them. A Do Not Resuscitate order (DNR) is typically made in conjunction with your loved one's doctor.

If you have a DNR order, keep it handy where you can grab it quickly. When paramedics arrived at my grandmother's home to transport her to hospital on what would be her final admission, I gave them the DNR order in case her heart stopped while being transported by ambulance.

As your loved one nears the time of his or her death, ask the palliative care team to provide you with information on what to do and who to contact should your loved one die at home. Death can have its own timetable and being informed is important even though you may be 'planning' on your loved one dying in hospital. Occasionally, a loved one dies in their sleep at home and you'll need to know what to do should that occur. The more you know, the better prepared you'll be for whatever comes your way.

In addition, find out your loved one's wishes following his or her death. Does your loved one want a funeral or a quiet informal get-together? Would they prefer to be buried or cremated? Does he or she want their ashes interred or scattered? Although not a pleasant line of questioning, the answers are important to know. Make sure family and friends are also aware of your loved one's final wishes. It's sad to discuss this subject while your loved one is still alive but knowing what his or her preferences are helps avoid possible family disagreements later as well as respecting his or her wishes.

9. Be Prepared to Rearrange Rooms and Furniture

As more assistive equipment is brought into the home, certain pieces of furniture may need to be rearranged or relocated. Your loved one may possibly react in some manner to these changes especially if you're caring for them in their own home. Explain to him or her the reason for the relocations.

It's also helpful to have items your loved one frequently uses within their easy reach. Make sure there's a small end table not only beside his or her bed but in any other room they frequent. Use this table for a box of tissues, a cup of water, eyeglasses, small snack, reading materials, and bell otherwise you'll be running back and forth throughout the day for these little things.

10. Ideas for Enjoyment

One of the most important and kind things you can do as a caregiver is ensure your loved one experiences as much good cheer and psychological comfort as possible in the face of their worsening illness. Entertaining and engaging activities have a calming effect and help relieve anxiety. Break up the hours of your loved one's long day by periodically diverting their mind off their disease. Your loved one is still alive and will benefit from learning new things, laughing, and being creatively challenged in a light-hearted, fun way. These activities are good for you too and done together may become some of the warmest memories you hold dear once your caregiving days are over. Find out what your loved one enjoys.

Here are a few ideas:
- o Read books or magazines together.
- o Share family stories, perhaps something funny that happened to you both.
- o Browse photo albums.
- o Watch movies, television programs, sport matches, or documentaries.

- Play your loved one's favorite music or listen to Talk Radio.
- Play games such as cards, dominos, or board games such as checkers. Playing games is something visitors can do with your loved one as well.
- Work on a puzzle together. There are many puzzles available from easy to challenging, small or large.
- Work on fun arts & crafts projects depending upon your loved one's interests and abilities.
- Invite visitors over if your loved one feels well enough for it. Socializing is good for his or her mental and emotional state. Stimulating conversation and laughter are good for you too. Keep in mind however, that such visits can also tax your loved one's energy so be sure not to overdo it.
- Adult coloring books are quite popular and come in many different themes and sizes. There's bound to be one your loved one would enjoy. Consider buying two books and color together. Coloring will relax both of you and provide an opportunity to chat about other things outside of sickness.
- Take short walks or wheelchair excursions outside in the fresh-air. Looking at plants, hearing birds sing, feeling warm sunshine, or a gentle breeze is an enjoyable experience for someone confined indoors most of the day.

One my grandmother's friends showed Nana the games she had on her iPad. Nana seemed interested so I bought her a small tablet and downloaded several games onto it for her. She enjoyed it so much that she played endlessly the day it arrived and inadvertently strained her wrist! Afterall, she was elderly with osteoporosis in her bones. At first, I felt terrible for not realizing Nana was overdoing it but later we laughed about it. Her friends and I teased her mercilessly after that by referring to her wrapped wrist as her 'sports injury!' I had to monitor her game playing after that!

11. *Enlist the Help of Family and Friends*

Enlist a reliable family member or friend to pass along pertinent news regarding your loved one when you're unable do so. Communicating daily to multiple people can become extremely time-consuming particularly towards the end of your loved one's life and especially if you're the sole caregiver.

In addition, helpful friends or family who can assist with groceries and other necessary items makes a difference. Julius Caesar wasn't referring to cucumbers and toilet paper when he advised his men to "Divide and conquer" but the general idea works well in caregiving.

Family may also be willing to sit with your loved one occasionally so you can have respite.

Let family and friends know that your needs and those of your loved one will change as time progresses. You may need to elicit their help in different ways over the long haul

12. *Other Things to Consider*

Help your loved one write letters, send cards, or make phone calls to family and friends whenever he or she feels up to it and wishes to do so. It's important for him or her to feel connected to those they care about especially on holidays and birthdays. Nana was in tears the night of Christmas Eve when she realized she didn't have a gift for a much-loved friend. It wasn't her fault. Nana was too unwell to go out and shop for something. I was tired and had forgotten. I felt awful watching the tears roll down Nana's face. This is another thing you can ask family and friends to help with.

Strength doesn't come
From what you can do,
It comes from overcoming
The things you thought you couldn't.

Author Unknown

In closing, you are a caregiver embarking upon a journey in which only the ending is known and the finale of your loved one's story will break your heart. Witnessing the one you care for slowly succumb to their illness is emotionally painful. Nothing between now and then is likely to play out as you might imagine. But keep in mind there will be many meaningful and joyful moments along the way for you to cherish.

Don't be reluctant to ask for help when you need it. You'll need to vent your emotions occasionally and so will your loved one. Share your concerns and feelings with someone you trust and are comfortable with. If you're unable to find anyone who fits the bill, contact the palliative care team. Above all, remember, you aren't alone. Support is out there and those of us who have been or who are caregivers, carry you close in our thoughts and prayers as you walk your loved one Home.

Torie Cooper

Chapter 2

You the Caregiver: No Batteries, Love Powered

*The heart will break,
But broken live on.*

Lord Byron

Nothing in my life prior to caregiving, truly prepared me to dress and undress my grandmother, change her disposable underwear, and wipe her bottom. I didn't anticipate coaxing her as you would a child to take medicine that didn't taste good. Giving her a wash, shaving her chin, cutting her toenails, placing rollers in her hair, or cutting her food into tiny pieces to minimize choking, were tasks I hadn't rehearsed. I had no foundation that readied me to hold thick feminine hygiene pads against Nana's bottom in an effort to stop rectal bleeding caused by an angry tumor. Neither was I ready for the sadness of communicating with her through short handwritten notes when her vocal cords became too weak for speaking. Most of my family tended to die with little warning, giving me no experience in caring for a terminally ill loved one.

Caregiving was a new world for me. It was as foreign as walking on the surface of Mars. Much of the time I was sad, afraid, and lost. As my grandmother came to depend increasingly upon me, so I became increasingly dependent upon the palliative care team and community nurses for guidance, information, and support. When my caregiving days ended, I realized that nothing else I might ever do in life would be as meaningful as being my grandmother's caregiver. To this day, I'm still learning and growing from that powerful experience.

Emotions and Stress

As caregivers, we are dropped by parachute into a medical war zone. Occasionally, our loved ones may negotiate a temporary truce with their illness but they won't win the war. These are challenging times and as caregivers, it's common for us to feel our emotions are being held hostage until our loved one's body surrenders and a doctor or nurse declares the war over.

Whatever you feel in any given moment, don't be too hard on yourself. Give yourself as much psychological space as you can. Watching someone you love slowly deteriorate is heartbreaking. As his or her caregiver, you will live with feelings of helplessness, knowing you cannot change the outcome of your loved one's story. Stress becomes a constant companion, a shadow you cannot outrun. You may find yourself moving through an emotional gauntlet confronting sadness, depression, anger, guilt, and grief.

As caregivers, we have genuine needs of our own; emptiness that requires filling. We aren't machines made of steel and aluminum. We need understanding, not grease. Support, not oil. The great challenge of caregiving involves smoothing our own side of the path in addition to our loved one's as we walk by their side. If you place your loved one upon pavement while you struggle over ruts, rocks, and loose gravel, you're going to grow weary and trip. It's only a matter of time. Along with your loved one, make yourself a priority.

Be aware of conflicting thoughts and emotions that may arise. As an example, it was during the Christmas season that I most missed family members back in the U.S. While in the supermarket, I fought back tears listening to Christmas carols playing over the speaker system. Bing Crosby singing, *I'll be Home for Christmas* really turned on the waterworks! A psychologist specializing in caregiving and family issues once remarked to me, "It must be emotionally hard for you Torie because going back home means your grandmother has to die." Her comment really struck me and brought into focus many of the mixed feelings and guilt I struggled with. I realized I needed to make peace with seemingly opposing thoughts and emotions. I could miss my family and also want to be by my grandmother's side. I could want the hardships of caregiving to end while also not wanting Nana to die.

You too, may have conflicting thoughts and emotions while caregiving. It's common to feel like a human tennis ball being struck by outside forces from one side of life's court to the other. Don't be too hard on yourself whenever an emotional Wimbledon takes place.

In addition, you may periodically cry, out of sheer frustration for the things you miss; for the way your life has changed since you began caregiving. Here are a few possible examples for the source of those tears:

- o The distressing nature of looking after someone you love whose time on earth is limited.
- o You have no social life, feel lonely, and isolated.
- o You simply want one night's worth of uninterrupted sleep.
- o You want to eat a hot meal without being disturbed.
- o Family and friends frequently call on the phone or knock on the door without realizing you're in the middle of taking your loved one to the toilet and changing their

underwear. They continue calling or knocking until you pick up the phone or answer the door, dead on your feet.
- You cook a meal your loved one normally enjoys only to have them push their plate away telling you they no longer like it. Now you must start all over and cook something else even though you're bone tired and will have twice as many pots and pans to wash later.
- You rarely have a moments' peace just for yourself.
- Others who have never been caregivers may not understand what you're going through and inadvertently say things that hurt rather than help.
- Your lower back is killing you, as you watch the slow-motion trajectory of a pill that your loved one has dropped as it falls to the ground and rolls. You wonder whether you can even stoop to pick it up, you're so tired and sore.
- You'll wonder when your life will ever go back to normal, quickly realizing your life will never be what it once was. Someone you dearly love is dying and this caregiving experience is changing you.

Thankfully, you can also anticipate many wonderful feel-good moments on your caregiving journey. When you least expect it, there'll be funny moments and numerous occasions in which your heart melts at the kindness of others including your loved one.

For example, my grandmother always thanked me when I took her to the bathroom or organized her medications. She was a grateful person by nature. It was one of the things I loved about her. Softly she'd say, "You're so good to me." Any upset I may have been harboring would melt away at the sound of her quiet voice. Her gratitude in the face of vulnerability deeply touched me.

> *Sometimes I go about*
> *Pitying myself*
> *And all the while*
> *I am being carried by great winds*
> *Across the sky.*

Ojibway Saying

The Relationship Between You and Your Loved One

The quality of the relationship between you and your loved one affects how you feel about being their caregiver. As Elise NeeDell Babcock stated so well in her book, *When Life Becomes Precious*, "Whatever your situation, as the primary caregiver you are the one who has to take the brunt of the patient's emotions. And if the relationship has problems, as many do, these problems will be exacerbated by the stress you will both be under."

Caring for the relationship between you and your loved one is as equally important as caring for your loved one's physical body and its needs. Encourage healing conversations, forgive anything that needs to be forgiven. Endeavor to understand the way the illness has affected each of you. One of you is gradually losing independence and facing imminent death. The other is becoming decision-maker, nurse, cook, cleaner, and minister on-call 24/7. Both of you are grieving what has already been lost and what is yet to be taken, and desperately trying to accept that harsh reality. Build a bridge between one another not a wall. If you need assistance contact the palliative care team or a community counsellor. You won't save a life but you may save a relationship.

Occasionally, I failed at hiding my frustrations from my grandmother. These upsetting moments led her to believe she was being a bother. Later, I felt terrible for not controlling my emotions better. I'd tell myself that I must be an awful granddaughter! Of course, I wasn't. I was doing everything in my power to look after Nana. I loved her and maintained a positive attitude overall but sometimes I was simply having a bad day. Following these moments, I'd apologize and explain that I was just a little tired. I told my grandmother I loved her and didn't want to be anywhere else but by her side caring for her. On the inside however, I acknowledged I needed more help.

Uncomfortable moments such as these in which one of you expresses frustration will occur regardless of the relationship's strength. Although unpleasant, irritations are a normal part of caregiving, of being human and not machine. In healthy relationships, this friction can be used to draw closer to one another and gain better understanding of how each of you is feeling and being impacted by the illness.

An important way of maintaining a respectful and compassionate relationship is through open dialogue. Be honest with one another and encourage awareness. Our loved ones either willingly or unwillingly, offer themselves up to us to be cared for. That isn't easy. As caregivers we must see our own vulnerability within theirs. Why not discover and appreciate each other while traveling Homeward?

Monitor Your Own Well-being

Both your mental and physical health will be challenged while caregiving. Any pre-existing conditions or tendencies you have may be exacerbated. If you're under a doctor's care it's important to continue and to let your doctor know you are now a caregiver. Caring for a terminally ill loved one is a difficult occupation. Stressed and worn out, each day will siphon your energy until your body and mind is similar to a car without petrol; an empty shell, running only on fumes.

During my early days and weeks as a caregiver, I was tired without realizing how much more worn out and stressed I was to become. As time passed, my fatigue increased and soon my ability to think with the clarity of pre-caregiving days vanished. Towards the end I became exhausted. Prior to being a caregiver,

I never knew what true exhaustion was. Shamefully, I used to wonder about people who were hospitalized with exhaustion – why didn't they just go to bed earlier? I really didn't get it. Now I do. Exhaustion is unhealthy and unsafe. Attempting to care for your loved one while exhausted is a losing battle for both of you. Please don't allow yourself to slip into that place.

Sleep-deprivation combined with continual stress can lead not only to poor decision-making, but unhealthy eating habits and a weakened immune system, not to mention mental train wrecks. How can we provide our loved one with the quality of care they deserve when we are in this condition? Ideally, your mental and physical health must be viewed as having equal value to that of your loved one's needs. Unfortunately, as caregivers, we frequently operate under less than ideal circumstances. Even so, care for yourself as much as possible. This isn't selfishness, it's about being the best caregiver you're able to be. Your loved one needs you to be well.

Admittedly, it's difficult not to fall through cracks that grow ever wider. At first, we don't notice them. They're small and although tired, we feel we'll manage somehow. As greater fatigue encroaches, the cracks widen. This is when we risk neglecting our own needs for those of our loved one. We're similar to an airplane on autopilot mindlessly making the motions. This is the time to listen to the concerns of the palliative care team (if not before!). Often, they see what we cannot. These professionals look at our situation from a place of objectivity and see the bigger picture. Listen to their recommendations and suggestions.

Caregiving becomes more demanding as our loved one's illness progresses. I was sore and aching from lifting my grandmother throughout the day. Although she was a small lady, Nana became heavier as her muscles weakened. In fact, she was surprisingly heavy even though she was losing body mass. Worried about injuring my back, occupational therapists from Nana's hospital suggested assistive equipment to help me shift her from place to place more easily. They came to our home demonstrated methods of caring for her that were safer for my spine.

Towards the very end of my grandmother's life, the short walk to and from her mailbox became the only aerobic exercise I received each day. Sleeping through the night was no longer possible due to Nana's around the clock needs. Drinking five cups of tea or coffee a day – often cold – was a must to prevent me from literally laying on the floor where I stood and collapsing into desperately needed sleep. Eventually, I could no longer read books or watch a television program from start to finish. I was never off-duty. Towards the end of my caregiving experience, I took showers infrequently because it was too risky to leave my grandmother alone even for a few minutes. Thankfully, it was winter at that point and too cold for me to get grubby. Nana had lost all bowel control and getting her into the one bathroom we shared was a priority for quickly changing her undergarments. I also couldn't sit at the kitchen table and enjoy a hot meal. The only time I could cook for myself and eat a meal from beginning to end was whenever Nana was in hospital. Otherwise, I wasn't eating well and for the most part snacking upon what I could grab quickly. I was too tired to cook and the thought of cleaning dirty dishes afterwards really did me in! I often wore the same wrinkled clothes over and over; everyone told me I looked terrible.

I can do this I thought.
And even if I can't, I have to.

Author Unknown

Making Mistakes

You'll make mistakes while caregiving. Like most things in life, we learn as we go and we learn best from errors and hardship. It's virtually impossible to think straight and not blunder while sleep deprived. On top of that, the relentless emotional strain involved with the inevitable loss of our loved one only adds fuel to the fire.

As caregivers, we are flawed and wounded; heart-bound to care for those who are flawed, wounded, and unwell. Mistakes are par for the course.

Balancing Communication with Family and Friends

Communicating with family and friends about your loved one's current condition versus spending quality time with your loved one can be a juggling act at times. Family and friends deserve to know how you and your loved one are managing. They too, are concerned and upset at the thought of losing the person they love. However, in between making and receiving phone calls and emails, a significant chunk of time can be torn from the fabric of your day. It helps to have a willing friend assist you in communicating with everyone especially as your loved one deteriorates.

I was in Australia six months before purchasing a small computer tablet onto which I downloaded games for my grandmother to play. This tablet also became the primary means by which I communicated with family in America and a few in Australia who were difficult to round-up by phone. One afternoon, my grandmother made an innocent comment about me always being on the computer. I felt badly! Often when using the tablet, Nana was sitting near me in her chair with her eyes closed. I had assumed she was dozing off. Apparently, at least some of the time she was simply closing her eyes. Those were moments I could have spent with her – talking, laughing, playing a game, or watching a movie together. Clearly, I had missed precious opportunities to be with my grandmother. Did she feel neglected? Bored? Her comment troubled me.

Be prepared for issues such as this especially if you're the sole caregiver as I was. You won't always get it right but do the best you can. Of course, this situation partly depends upon the size of your family and number of friends. Also keep in mind that balance is never stagnant but fluctuates with change. Balance is a person teetering on a tightrope between two buildings. Welcome to life as a caregiver!

> *Count each day as a separate life.*
>
> Seneca

Divided Days and Quality Time

Your days as a caregiver will typically be divided into repeated segments revolving around medications, meals, and toileting. These tasks will flow from one to the other with each taking longer than you might imagine. In between, there are phone calls to make and receive, visitors (announced and unannounced), prescriptions to be placed or meds picked up from the pharmacist, nails trimmed, hair washed, bathroom accidents cleaned up, groceries bought, bathroom garbage removed two or three times a day due to soiled disposable underwear, clothes washed, and soiled bedsheets changed. In between these tasks, you'll attempt to spend quality time with your loved one.

While it's not my intention to frighten you with a litany of difficulties, knowing what may possibly lie ahead is important so that you can better prepare for it. Acquiring information as opposed to being blind-sided translates into less stress. Also, if you're fortunate to share caregiving duties with another person, then that alone will help you enormously.

Leaving Your Brain Behind

You may be surprised at how absent-minded you become as a caregiver. Let me share my beach adventure with you. My sister Renee was visiting from America and wanted time alone with our grandmother. She also knew I could use a break. Being a warm day, Renee suggested I go to the beach. So off I went, taking a bus and then a train to the beachside town of Cronulla.

Arriving midday, I walked down to the waterfront and bought piping hot fish 'n chips and a cold bottle of Bundaberg ginger beer to wash them down with. Sitting upon a grassy hill overlooking the sea and eating my lunch beneath stately Norfolk pines was just what I needed. I soaked up the sights and sounds of people, ocean, and squawking seagulls. It was wonderful! I took it all in as if trying to make the moment last forever. I especially enjoyed the spaciousness of it all. More importantly, there was no sign of illness anywhere. Before long I forgot about everything back at Nana's house. I was in seventh heaven!

Following my salty meal, I walked down to the beach. Feeling warm sand between my toes and a cool breeze blowing through my hair felt amazing! Families were everywhere with children splashing in the shallows, building sand castles, or clinging to boogie boards. The ebb and flow of the ocean was mesmerizing as it washed playfully across my feet and ankles. Once in a while a larger wave surged past my knees. I felt such joy and exuberance! This is when I made the fateful decision to enter the water fully clothed. If being up to my knees in water felt good, how much better would it feel if I went all the way in? Besides, other people had t-shirts on over their bathing suits, perhaps no-one would notice I wasn't wearing any swimming attire at all. So in I went with full abandon! It was absolutely glorious! I dove beneath the refreshing waves, flipped onto my back, and then dove again. I was a virtual human seal!

Not surprisingly, I lost track of time but eventually called it a day. Trudging out of the water, I looked like a sunburned version of *The Creature from the Black Lagoon!* That's precisely the moment it occurred to me that I had no beach towel in my possession! I couldn't even wipe my nose let alone the rest of me! Then I remembered, there had been beach towels for sale on tabletops outside of a few stores I'd passed earlier. My plan was to walk back and buy one. Off I went down the street looking like a wet mop, dripping past people sitting at outdoor restaurants and cafes. Coming to a shop selling towels I realized I had barely any money with me - not even enough for a cheap beach towel. Apparently, I had spent all my money on lunch. Not to worry, a light bulb in my brain suddenly lit up - I could use my credit card. What relief! Thank goodness for plastic! But then I discovered I'd brought a different wallet with me and this one didn't have my credit card in it. Ugh!

Thankfully, at least I did have the means to return to Nana's home using my Opal transportation card. I hopped onto the next train trying not to think about my shoddy appearance. As I was absolutely drenched, I knew it'd be inconsiderate to sit down and get the train seat wet. So I stood and held onto a vertical rail. More and more people got onto the train each time it stopped. I kept my sunglasses on to conceal my identity (embarrassment) and tried to avoid eye contact with my fellow passengers. Glancing down at my feet, I was horrified to discover a large puddle of seawater had collected beneath me and parts of my feet and lower legs were covered in a layer of wet sand. Water was dripping off my hair and clothes. I looked like something a cat would drag in on a stormy night! I was mortified and counting the stops until I could get off the train. Eventually I exited with great relief only to remember I wasn't home yet. I still had a bus to catch!

Climbing the bus steps, I was greeted by strange looks and made my way to the back. Still soggy, I sat on the very edge of the seat balancing myself precariously. Once again, I avoided eye contact with other travelers. Suddenly, I heard a woman in a loud voice ask, "You been to the beach?" I could have cringed! I looked up and discovered the voice belonged to a nice lady I was acquainted with. I proceeded to give her and other curious passengers a brief explanation for my water-logged condition! They seemed to enjoy the story.

Looking back on it now, it's an amusing tale that illustrates what can happen to any caregiver. Given a moment of respite, who knows what we'll do with it! We run off like toddlers living in the moment without consequences - not able to properly think things through or connect the dots. Perhaps we shouldn't go off alone. Perhaps we need our own caregiver; someone who can stop us from dancing naked on a table-top at a local pub or going sky-diving without a parachute!

> *Caring is being there*
> *When you want to be somewhere else.*
>
> Author Unknown

Grief Begins Prior to Death

Did Nana know how much she meant to me? I wasn't sure she could grasp how hard it was to watch her slowly die but I also didn't want her to carry that burden. Often, as my grandmother rocked gently back and forth upon her squeaky chair, I felt such a deep sense of loss; grieving for her while she was still alive. Often, I tried to hold back my tears and hide my sorrow. I wasn't sure whether to share my feelings with her. I didn't want my sadness to cause her to worry about me and how I would cope when she was gone. Sometimes, I found something that needed doing in another room and wiped my tears. I felt as though I were trying to hold back the ocean.

There were occasions however, in which my grandmother did see me cry. She'd tell me that when she passes away, she will always watch over me. I never knew how much time I had left with Nana and not knowing played upon my anxiety. Waiting day in and day out, for the end to come was nerve-wracking.

While caring for your loved one, you too may find yourself overcome with emotion and like me, having to decide whether or not to leave the room. Expect these moments. They'll be plenty of them and know that it's alright to cry. Anticipatory grief is normal under the circumstances. Watching your loved one deteriorate, wondering *when* they'll pass away, and waiting day after day for that dreaded moment to arrive, is a huge contributor to the stress you'll feel as their caregiver.

Impending loss is similar to water continually dripping upon stone. With time, the stone wears down, changing shape. Each day, the forecast of future grief releases a drop of sorrow upon your shoulders. Some days that drop will have more weight to it than other days. Is there an umbrella that can protect caregivers from the dripping waters of anticipatory grief? No, but we can learn to co-exist with emotional pain, accept its presence, and make peace with being 'wet.' Discuss your feelings with the palliative care team. Support is available. Find comfort in the knowledge that with small steps, taken in a healthy direction, you can weather these daily droplets of sorrow.

Supermarket Holiday

You might be surprised at the ordinary places in your neighborhood that will transform themselves into glorious holiday destinations as caregiving swallows more and more of your time.

For me, excursions to the supermarket became dreamlike vacations. They were breaks from caregiving. Who could imagine that confectionary, biscuit, and bread aisles could be so mesmerizing with their multi-colored wrappers and boxes? Who knew the aroma of fresh prawns, rotisserie chicken, and passionfruit could mentally transport me to exotic locales? I loved the supermarket!

You too, will come to regard the supermarket with affection. It's a place where no-one speaks about sickness, death, or hospitals. So enjoy the pretty shades of lavender and green found on hand-made bars of soap and the alluring names of herbal teas and coffee. Admire the texture of crumpets and the stately dairy cows pictured on cartons of milk. Your mind and body will relish the break.

Life Happens While Caregiving

There is never a good time for an object to break or for something to go wrong. When you're caregiving these frustrating occurrences can feel worse. Never assume everything around you will remain hunky dory while looking after your loved one. A car tire may go flat, the washing machine break down, or you accidentally sit on your glasses. Life isn't always fair and you need these bumps in the road as much as you need an ingrown toenail! Roll with life's punches as best you can. If you need additional help with a problematic situation, ask for assistance especially if whatever has taken place directly affects your ability to care for your loved one.

For example, an oven switch broke one morning and I couldn't cook until a repairman came to fix it. On another occasion, the one and only light bulb in the bathroom blew and was located too high for me to reach it. Not having a ladder, I had to wait for a handyman to arrive with one. Shortly thereafter, the telephone decided not to work. Let me tell you, from one caregiver to another, that when the telephone doesn't work, your family and friends will worry. In their minds, something awful has surely happened – either your loved one is dying in hospital, an old Russian satellite has fallen from the sky onto your house, or a lion has escaped the zoo and is sitting in front of you both and drooling! Yes, when the telephone fails to function, every person you know including your 6th cousin twice removed, shows up at the front door to make sure that you and your loved one are alright! The list goes on.

Unpleasant or irritating events don't stop because your loved one has cancer or because you haven't slept well. Be prepared for the inconvenience and again, ask for additional assistance if you need it.

Caregiver's Guilt

Following your caregiving journey, you may find yourself wondering what you could have done differently or more effectively to smooth the rough edges of your dear one's path. Please remember that what you did or didn't do, the decisions you made, represented your best effort at the time. It's not easy to let go of "I should have…," "I wish…," and "If only…" But do make a conscious effort to release yourself from any regrets or feelings of guilt. You don't deserve the suffering these feelings bring. In order to heal, you must accept your strengths and weaknesses within the landscape of the circumstances you found yourself in. Will you be more effective in the future should you become a caregiver again? Absolutely. You've learned and you've grown. This is how our best gets better and we evolve into stronger, more compassionate human beings.

Caregiving taxes you
But it also transforms you.

Author Unknown

Practical Tips

An unspoken definition of 'caregiver' seems to involve a person who neglects him or herself for the good of another. There's a simple reason for that – it's true! Why do we as caregivers so often neglect our own needs? Perhaps we don't begin that way but with passing time our loved one increasingly depends upon us and ever so slowly, we forget ourselves. We toss long, flowing capes over our shoulders and attempt to do it all! We love our special someone and love *gives*. But we must save some of that love, some of that giving for ourselves too. Here are a few suggestions, in no particular order, for looking after yourself:

1. Get a Haircut

Getting my hair cut wasn't easy, especially as Nana's condition deteriorated and I could no longer leave her alone. At times I resembled some wild woman who had stumbled out of the jungle! Fortunately, a local hairdresser who worked with housebound clients and had been cutting Nana's hair at home, kindly agreed to cut mine as well. Keeping my hair regularly trimmed made a big difference to how I felt. I believe the neighbors also appreciated me not looking like a Himalayan yak! Sometimes the smallest and simplest thing such as getting a haircut can really make a caregiver feel good.

2. Spend Time in Nature

Whenever you can, spend a quiet moment in nature. Unless you're being chased by a tiger, the natural world is very healing. If your loved one is well enough to sit outside in the sun, sit together and enjoy the warmth of sunlight upon your skin. Listen to birds sing, watch colorful butterflies flutter about, and smell the sweet fragrance of flowers. Even short periods of time outdoors will do you the world of good.

3. Buy Small Books that Open Anywhere

Shortly after arriving in Australia, I bought two small books filled with encouraging quotes and poems. I could pick up either book and turn to any page for instant inspiration. Reading the compassionate words of others helped me feel a little less lonely. I especially enjoyed reading something positive and comforting while traveling by train to visit Nana whenever she was in hospital. Consider buying a few books to have available when you need a mental boost. Your loved one might also appreciate reading them too.

4. Find People Who Will Listen

With all the frustrations and emotions that revolve around caring for a terminally ill loved one, you'll need to find someone you can talk to. Make use of trusted family members, friends, and the palliative care team. Failing to release pent up feelings can easily transform you into a stick of human dynamite. It won't take much to light the fuse. Be kind to yourself and take every opportunity to release emotions and vent frustrations to someone willing to lend you their ears. You'll feel so much better afterwards.

5. Find Humor

Remember to look for humorous moments and enjoy a good laugh. One evening, having dozed off into fitful, unsatisfying slumber, I rolled over only to suddenly awaken with a crash! I had rolled off the bed and onto the floor behind my grandmother's rocking chair! Not since childhood had I fallen out of bed. I couldn't believe it! I laid there for a moment stunned, with my arms, legs, and body wrapped tightly in a twisted sheet and blanket. I resembled an Egyptian mummy – a disheveled Queen Nefertiti perhaps?! Tired, part of me contemplated remaining on the floor for the rest of the night while the other part thought I should get up, survey any damages, and crawl back into bed. The latter won over. Soon afterwards, Nana rang her bedside bell for bathroom assistance. I told her about falling out of bed and we both had a good laugh. She offered to lend me her bed rail!

Appreciate the funny side of your caregiving experiences whenever you can. Despite the seriousness of caring for a terminally ill loved one, there'll be many amusing moments as well. Laughter is another release valve for relieving pent up stress. As a caregiver, you'll need to use all the tools in your toolbox when it comes to self-maintenance.

6. Eat and Drink Well

Eat and drink as nutritiously as you're able. Consult your doctor regarding vitamins or supplements. Don't let yourself get too run down. I did and wouldn't recommend it. Check the supermarket for protein shakes, juice drinks, and health foods.
It's too easy to grab snacks rather than take the necessary time for ourselves. As caregivers, we're so tired but do need to regularly put the best food, drinks, or healthy snacks into our body.

Also, don't neglect your annual flu vaccine. This will protect both yourself and your loved one. Unfortunately, there is much ignorance and misunderstanding surrounding vaccines. Talk with your doctor or pharmacist.

7. Turn on the Television or Radio Occasionally

Playing music in the background while going about your day can have a relaxing effect upon stressed nerves. It doesn't matter if it's Mozart or the Rolling Stones as long as it lifts your spirits. Make sure the music isn't bothering your loved one though. If the floor boards are shaking and your loved one's dentures have come loose, then the music is probably too loud! You can also have a television program turned on while working. Sometimes the sound of other voices can help you feel a little less lonely. There'll be days in which you'll long to hear voices that aren't discussing illness, medications, or bowel movements.

<u>Conversation Starters</u>

Below, are a few suggestions for conversations you may choose to have with your loved one during the course of his or her illness. Certainly, you don't have to discuss any of these subjects if you feel uncomfortable. If nothing else, these conversation starters will likely resonate with you as you navigate a field of never-ending tasks and unexpected detours.

What I Would Like My Loved One to Know:

~ Sometimes I'm on the phone talking with a family member, friend, or member of the palliative care team and wonder if you can hear me speaking with them. I wonder if you overhear me talking about the progression of your illness, predictions of your passing, and what the end might possibly bring. I fear you may overhear me tell others that I'm tired and struggling to stay afloat. I worry you'll think you're being a burden to me. You are . . . you're a burden of love.

~ Please trust me when I recommend using a piece of safety or mobility equipment such as a walker. Trust that I see something you may not, something from a different perspective. I notice your increasing instability. Your muscles aren't quite as strong as they once were. I worry you may fall and hurt yourself.

~ Sometimes I'm so terribly busy looking *after* you that I forget to be *with* you. I want to appreciate you and thank you for all you've done for me. I want to take in all your precious details; the sound of your gentle voice, your shiny blue eyes, the feel of your soft hair, the clean smell of the lotion you put on your face. I want to hold your hand and savor its warmth. I want to share stories and laughter, perhaps even cry together. I want to find ways to be present with you even though there are always tasks to complete.

~ I realize you may see _____ (fill in the blank) as one more indignity, a reminder of your continuing loss of independence. But it would really help me if you would wear disposable undergarments (for example) or _____ (fill in the blank) from now on. It's not easy for me to wash and dry underwear, pants, pajamas, nightgowns, bedsheets, chair cushions as often as I do. It pains me to bring this up. It's not your fault there are accidents, it's your disease. Wearing disposable undergarments or _____ (fill in the blank) would make each day much more comfortable for you as well. I want you to be comfortable, dry, and clean.

~ There are moments in which you feel relatively good and would probably like to play cards with me or do some other activity together. But sometimes I'm so worn out that I don't ask if you'd like to do something. Afterwards, I feel guilty for not taking advantage of the opportunity and I wonder if there'll be another one.

~ I don't want to place you in a nursing facility. I'd much rather you remain in your own home. But I'm the only person caring for you around the clock and it's becoming hard on me. Physically, I'm approaching my limits. If I can't look after you, we may not have a choice. Looking on the positive side, if you were in nursing home, we'd be able to spend quality time together rather than me being busy with so many other tasks. We'd have more time for stories, reading, and watching television together. My mind and body wouldn't be so broken.

~ Sometimes I wonder if I'm adequately addressing the feelings you may have about your own passing and your spiritual beliefs regarding this. You tell me that you "want to go" but I wonder whether there is any fear. Although you tell me there isn't, I'm not always sure. Perhaps I'm projecting my own feelings onto you.

~ I worry I may not be the best person to look after you. In some ways, I'm suited for caregiving but in other ways not. I worry whether I can give you the quality care you deserve.

~ I want you to know how proud I am of you. You've been through so much with your illness. Increasingly, the independence you once enjoyed has been taken from you yet you don't complain. You remain kind and loving. You keep things in perspective. You have become a teacher for me, mentoring me on how to live and die well. You've taught me that true dignity and independence are on the inside.

~ I'm concerned for your safety. You may not realize it but there are things you do that I feel are unsafe or have the potential to become unsafe. Sometimes you turn on the wrong controls for the stove or oven. Sometimes you forget to lock the door or you lean over too far to pick something up or step up onto a stool when you shouldn't. If you hurt yourself, it may mean I can no longer care for you at home (or worse). Please trust my judgement when it comes to your safety.

~ I'm concerned you feel troubled about me caring for you. Sometimes you say that I'm "ruining my life" by leaving my job and home in order to look after you. You're concerned about me but also need me. Those two things aren't easy to reconcile. I don't want you to have any guilt or feel you're a terrible burden. Cancer is the burden not you. You are so much more than this disease-ravaged body, this body of old age. Your inner self is age-less and wonderful. That's the part of you I love.

~ Sometimes I secretly wish you would take a nap or sleep in longer so that I could either rest or work on something I can't do while you're awake and needing me. Later I feel guilty for having those thoughts. I don't want to wish you away.

~ Once in a while, I'd like to sit and have a cup of tea undisturbed unless you need me for something important like toileting, food, or pain medicine. I love you very much but at times I'm desperate for a quiet moment of peace. That doesn't mean I don't want to care for you, it only means that we both need to give and take during this challenging time.

~ I watch you become more tired with each passing day. Once, you only slept at night but now you take naps during the day. These naps are becoming more frequent and lasting longer. You fall asleep in your chair even when we have visitors. You often comment, "I don't know why I feel so tired?" I know why but choose not to tell you. "It's all those strong medications you take Nana," is my go-to reply. While this answer is partly true, your increasing fatigue is a sign your body is slowly shutting down. You're nearing the end of your life. I watch you sleep and feel such sorrow. Part of me wants to shake you awake so that we can do something together – anything. I almost want to remind you that your tired body will be sleeping forever so stay awake as long as you can, while you can. But I don't wake you up. I let you rest and I nurse my broken heart. I don't want you to suffer but I also don't want you to pass away. So often I'm torn.

~ Sometimes you ask me to do a lot of small things among the many larger tasks. Sometimes you call me to throw away a candy wrapper or used tissue. These are simple requests but I'm so overcome with fatigue that these tiny appeals become the straw that broke the camel's back. I need you to be mindful of my needs too and that small things can usually wait. Sometimes I need you to remember that I am no longer young myself.

~ We're both emotionally and physically tired but for different reasons. Sometimes I want this experience to end. Later I feel guilty for thinking that way. At other times, I try hard to push the thought of losing you from my mind. I hope that day never comes. I fear I won't be able to handle life without you. Then I feel guilty because having you live longer means you're enduring more suffering. No matter what I think or feel, I often end up feeling guilty. I'm thinking of myself. Yet I also know I'm giving so much of myself to you.

> *Courage is not*
> *having the strength to go on;*
> *it is going on when you*
> *don't have the strength.*
>
> Theodore Roosevelt

In closing, remember that as a caregiver you are not alone. You have brothers and sisters who are walking a similar path at this very moment. They are different ages and from different walks of life but all are caring for someone they love. There will be challenging days ahead but you are strong. With assistance, you can do this. Be mindful and take baby steps, one foot in front of the other. As Lao Tzu so beautifully wrote, "A journey of a thousand miles begins with a single step."

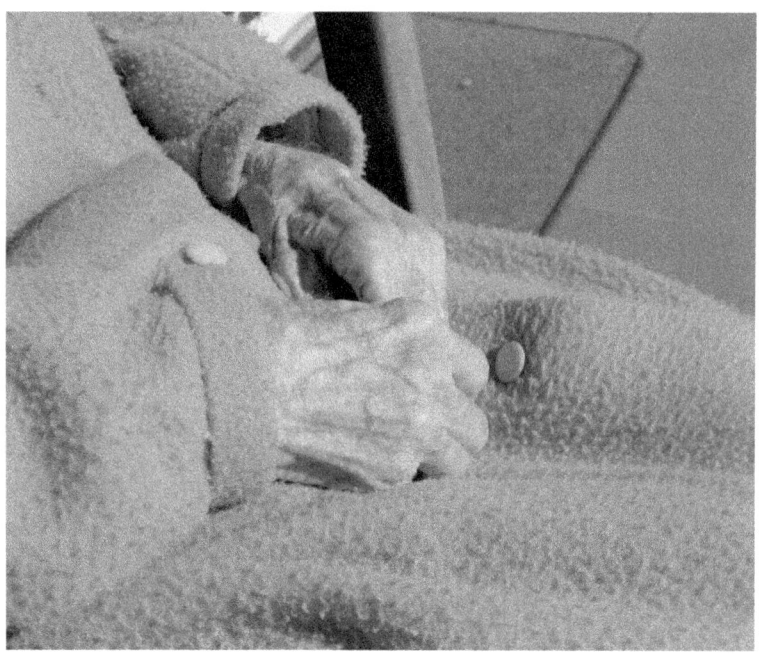

Chapter 3

The One You Are Caring For

*Out of a great need
We are all holding hands
And climbing.*

Hafiz

Early upon my caregiving journey, I found it difficult to hear my grandmother confide that she wanted to pass away. She mentioned this several times over the course of her illness. Her words sounded as though she were giving in or giving up in some way. I wanted to hear other words from her – not fighting words about beating cancer, after all she was 95 years old. But I yearned to hear something else. I wanted Nana to *want* to stay alive. I wanted her to want to live as long as possible and remain on this earth. I wanted her to want to be with me. Obviously, I was thinking of myself and how much I'd miss her. Not at all compassionate considering she was elderly and so unwell, but that was how I felt at the time. Perhaps my grandmother thought she was nothing but trouble. She wasn't of course, but I believe her words were at least partially derived from feelings of helplessness. Later, after caregiving, I came to better appreciate the myriad frustrations, indignities, and feelings of loss that a terminally ill person such as my grandmother may experience. I wish I'd had greater awareness of that when I began caregiving.

Our loved ones may experience varying degrees of grief over the loss of their physical and mental functions in addition to a perceived loss of purpose or meaning in life. Walking the final few steps of their life's journey, even with you by their side, is difficult and full of challenges. While it's hard to be a caregiver, we must always remember that it's hard being cared for. Our loved ones are forced to bear many burdens. They face loss of independence, privacy, possibly their home, and many decision-making abilities. Sharing one's vulnerability with another can be daunting. Furthermore, our loved ones face impending death with a clarity and realism the rest of us do not. Let us remind ourselves of this while caregiving. Let us look into our loved one's eyes and see our own vulnerability, our own suffering, and unite with them in compassion.

Transformation is the New Normal

Change. It's a small word with great significance for your loved one. He or she is enveloped by swirling winds of change over which they are powerless. As caregivers, awareness of the continual metamorphosis our loved one's experience can prompt us to reach deep within and draw upon our most compassionate selves. Channeling that consideration into kind words and actions, comforts and fortifies our loved ones.

Nana gradually lost muscle strength. This increasing weakness eventually impacted her ability to dress herself, walk without assistance, or cut her own food. As swallowing muscles became feeble, choking while eating and drinking became an issue. This also made it difficult for her to swallow her many medications. When Nana's vocal cords weakened, she was unable to speak above a bare whisper and had to write her thoughts and requests down on paper in order to communicate with me. Eventually, she could no longer wash herself without help. Nor could she wash her own clothes and hang them up to dry. She was unable to pour fresh water into a vase of flowers or sweep her small front porch. With failing eyesight reading became problematic. Although she wore a hearing aid, her hearing grew worse. Eventually, Nana could no longer hold the telephone receiver in her hands in order to speak with family or friends. She was unable to retrieve her mail. She couldn't take herself into the bathroom, get up or down from the toilet seat, or change her disposable underwear. She could no longer brush her hair properly. Nana's otherwise sharp mind was occasionally confused and forgetful. Whenever I was out of the house, neighbors told me she grew anxious until I returned. Two weeks before her passing, she could barely remove the dentures from her mouth in order to clean them.

Looking at the list of what were once simple tasks, it's easy to understand how terminally ill individuals can become depressed as they lose their ability to do even the smallest things for themselves. On top of this, loved ones living with a progressive disease such as cancer, often contend with pain and nausea. In my grandmother's case, colorectal cancer involved an increase in rectal bleeding along with a loss of bowel control. These circumstances are enormously impactful when placed upon the shoulders of a single individual. As tired as we might become as caregivers, we do well to contemplate what it must feel like to live on the receiving end of the assistance we give.

Awareness of Death

Intellectually, we all know we're going to die. However, receiving a diagnosis of terminal illness turns that knowledge into laser-focused awareness. Mortality becomes very real. This cognizance may result in a variety of emotions that cycle themselves around the hearts and minds of our loved ones like planets orbiting the sun. Even without consciously worrying, death may be simmering upon the backburner of his or her mind. Be sensitive to this and look for signs of anger, fear, sadness, or depression.

Your loved one's religious, spiritual, or philosophical beliefs will also play a significant role in how he or she views their inevitable passing. Even so, our loved ones may mourn life as they had known it and grieve for those they'll leave behind. He or she will miss the activities they once loved such as puttering around a garden, playing golf, or fishing. They will mourn important life events they may have wanted to attend such as births, weddings, and graduations. Your loved one may openly or quietly grieve these losses. Comfort him or her. Offer a listening ear and a hand to hold. Grieving the loss of their own lives is natural.

For many, gradual acceptance of death brings serenity and inner healing. Acceptance is a daily practice requiring conscious intention to that end. Our loved ones may accept their death in the morning only to fearfully fight it in the afternoon. Acceptance is a commitment of sorts and a psychological giving of permission. Permission for death to gently embrace us.

If, however, you notice that your loved one appears to be experiencing unwavering mental suffering, please contact the palliative care team. Pastoral care staff and counselors are invaluable sources of assistance as are representatives of your loved one's specific faith.

Sometimes, the things we can't change
End up changing us.

Author Unknown

Relationship in the Midst of Illness

Terminal illness can strain relationships. Let's revisit this important subject. If you and the person you're caring for shared a close bond before the illness, chances are you'll remain close. If the relationship had been poor, then the path ahead may be riddled with ruts and bumps. Caregiving within an environment of anger, blame, insults, unbridled fear, and demands is horrible for everyone. Fortunately, it's never too late for either of you to learn how to listen and share your feelings with one another no matter how painful. It's not too late to view the larger picture through the lens of sympathetic understanding.

If, as caregivers, we could read the inner history of the one we're caring for and know the path they have taken that has led them to this very moment, we'd probably discover enough fears, failures, tragedies, and disappointments to embrace them with a full heart. Our judgement of his or her words and actions, especially towards us, would likely drop from our hand like a heavy stone. Perhaps we might better understand and forgive angry, ungrateful outbursts aimed at us as caregivers. As long as you and the person in your care are both breathing, there is opportunity to write a new chapter together; to create a better ending to an old story. American philosopher and naturalist, Henry David Thoreau wrote, "The soft and tender roots of a plant can make their way through the hardest soil, even the cracks in a rock. Love works in the same way; nothing can resist love." Find love within yourself then share it with the person who is unwell.

Mental Confusion

It's not uncommon for terminally ill persons to experience mental confusion and forgetfulness. For that matter, confusion isn't uncommon in those of us who are otherwise healthy but post-menopausal either! Cognitive issues in a loved one present unique challenges in caring for them as their personal safety and possibly yours becomes a factor. Consult with the palliative care team if cognitive problems are of ongoing concern.

When I first arrived in Australia, I was saddened to find my grandmother mildly confused. She had always been so sharp-minded. Over the years, she often teased me for being forgetful and wondered how I made it through university! Nana's absent-mindedness upset me. I was afraid of losing a familiar part of her before she died and I didn't know whether her confusion would worsen. Fortunately, her jumbled mental state was intermittent. Nana would be her old self for weeks or months at a time and then suddenly have cognitive issues again. Whenever her mind was in a muddle, I never knew whether it was permanent or transient.

Confusion can reveal itself in many ways. Occasionally, Nana was upset with me over something she thought I had done but hadn't. With time, I learned not to take these comments personally. Confusion or mild irritability was Nana's cancer talking, not her.

As an example, a pastoral care worker from the hospital was visiting us and asked my grandmother how she felt about nursing homes. Nana didn't want to enter one and we all knew it. I was trying hard to keep her at home if possible. But Nana answered the question by pointing to me and declaring, "*She* wants me to go into one." I was stunned! I was on the front-line representing Nana's war on nursing homes and was her greatest defender. Sitting there, I couldn't believe what I was hearing. Our visitor shot a glance at me. We had often spoken privately regarding my grandmother's anti-nursing home stance. I leaned over and put my hand on Nana's arm, explaining to her that one of the reasons I was remaining in Australia was to help her stay at home. But her accusation rattled me even though she was obviously confused.

On another occasion my grandmother and I had family over for lunch. While there, one of them drove me to a nearby town to take care of an errand. When we returned, Nana had cleared the table and placed the dirty plates from our lunch in the bottom of a cupboard rather than near the kitchen sink to be washed. I didn't say anything to her when I discovered them but she had clearly been disoriented. At other times, Nana forgot how to use the remote control for her television even though she'd been using it for years. When I was away from the house, I'd call

Nana on the telephone to remind her to take her medications only to come home and find she hadn't taken them.

Emotionally prepare yourself should your loved one experience problems of thought, memory, and reasoning, especially if he or she becomes irritable and targets you. You're targeted because you're there. It can be upsetting in light of all you do for him or her but keep in mind the confusion and grouchiness isn't about you and it isn't who they really are. It's the illness talking.

Also keep in mind that cognitive issues can result in safety concerns. You may need to monitor your loved one closer. Ask for additional help if you need it. Always notify doctors and nurses if your loved one's mental condition changes.

Let Your Loved One Care for You

Early one afternoon, while away purchasing medications and supplies, I was overcome with an unexpected migraine. The sledgehammer pain, visual disturbances, and nausea quickly worsened as I climbed into the backseat of a taxi and dashed back to Nana's place. Entering her doorway, it was all I could do to put the bags on her table, take off my jacket, and collapse onto the daybed. Lying there, I wondered how I was going to look after Nana for the rest of the day. How was she going to remember to take her medications and cook food? I wondered whether this debilitating migraine was going to be the first of many to come. If that happened how would I continue to care for her? These worrisome thoughts didn't make me feel any better as I tried to find a way of working through my unpleasant symptoms. Suddenly, I felt something soft. Opening my eyes, I saw my little grandmother leaning over the bed, gently pulling a blanket up and over me. She slowly and carefully tucked it around my fetal-positioned body. Over the course of my life, there were countless times in which a similar scene had played out this way. Nana was a gentle and caring soul who had always been good to me and everyone else she knew. Although I worried about Nana having to fend for herself while I was bedridden, it also felt surprisingly comforting to have her there for me. She seemed more like the old Nana I knew. Perhaps looking after me that day helped her rally and be the strong one again.

My grandmother didn't drop dead because I was too sick to remind her to take her medications or because I couldn't cook for her. Fortunately, she was still able to take herself to the toilet at that point in her illness although she was unsteady and at risk for falls. But Nana managed to survive that afternoon. Looking back on it now, I wish I'd let her look after me more often. Later, this incident caused me to wonder whether I had taken over too many tasks too soon in caregiving.

Perhaps you too might find ways to allow your loved one to retain and experience a portion of their former role in relation to you. Even something as simple as asking for his or her advice on a particular subject might be helpful. Being on the receiving end of your loved one's kindness, knowledge, and experience gives him or her a sense of still being useful to you. Find opportunities for your loved one to be more of who they were prior to their illness. Let your loved one care for you once in a while. I'm sure he or she would love to do so.

You have within you
More love than you could
Ever understand.

Rumi

Not Wanting to Be a Bother

Occasionally, my grandmother would consider all I was doing for her and then attempt to do something she really couldn't or shouldn't do. This was done in a well-meaning effort not to bother me any more than necessary. Perhaps she also wanted to do something for herself for a change. Occasionally, Nana held off telling me she needed to use the bathroom until she was on the verge of losing control. She knew I was in the middle of another task and didn't want to interrupt me. It troubled me that Nana thought she was being such a nuisance. Holding off on bathroom visits wasn't good. Sometimes, she didn't make it.

Be mindful of your loved one doing something similar, especially when he or she notices you're busy doing multiple tasks. Let him or her know that using the bathroom or needing additional medication for pain or nausea always comes first no matter what else you're doing. You may need to repeatedly remind your loved one that he or she is not a bother to you, especially as their personal needs increase. Remind them that you're their caregiver because you love them and you want them to be comfortable above everything else you're doing.

Food Issues

Meals are a common and frustrating issue for caregivers. Prepare for and expect changes in your loved one's appetite and tastes. Your loved one may push back a plate of food that ordinarily he or she would have woofed down like a hungry puppy. Planning meals ahead of time becomes increasingly difficult as the changes occurring within your loved one's failing body result in fussiness.

As an example of maddening food issues, it was a hot day when my grandmother told me she felt like eating prawns for lunch. Thrilled that she could pinpoint something specific that she felt like eating, I raced outside on foot and down the steep hill to the supermarket. I grabbed a bag of fresh, tasty prawns and dashed back up the hill to Nana's place collapsing in a sweaty heap onto the nearest chair. My heart was pounding from the exertion. I recall wondering whether my grandmother realized I was now in my mid-50's and no longer had a 21-year old's body! Shaky from the effort in the blazing sun, I unwrapped the prawns and put them onto slices of bread. Suddenly, Nana looked down at the pink morsels and declared,

"This isn't what I wanted." What?! "This isn't what I wanted," she repeated. I could have hit her on top of the head with a brick! I told her she had indeed asked for prawns but she continued to deny it. Not wanting to push it further and upset her, I asked what she thought she had requested but she couldn't remember. With my fingers crossed I asked, "Nana, do you think you could eat these even if you had wanted something else?" She replied she didn't want them. Ugh! I was too hot and bothered to choke her so I fed her something else. After that, I learned to take Nana's gastronomic requests with a grain of salt and no longer raced out the door in the middle of a blistering summer day!

Sometimes, a change of scenery or a change in *chef* can make a difference to your loved one. My sister Renee flew from the U.S. to Australia for a good-bye visit. She and my grandmother had always been close. Nana seemed to rally at the news that Renee was coming to spend a few weeks with us. Prior to my sister's visit, I'd been having trouble finding food that Nana would eat. She'd either turn down my offerings or pick at her plate at best. But as soon as Renee began cooking every meal for us, Nana perked up and loved whatever was placed on the table in front of her! This was quite a dramatic change from my point of view. At first, I felt embarrassed that my culinary skills must obviously be atrocious compared to Renee's but then I realized it was nothing personal. It was about Nana enjoying her food for the first time in many months. On top of that, I was grateful to have someone cooking for me as well. I felt spoiled sitting down to my sister's wonderful meals.

Feeding your finicky loved one may challenge your patience but someday you and I will probably drive our own caregivers mad! Just remember your loved one is housed within a crumbling and changing body. Food that he or she once savored simply doesn't taste the same anymore. Have a variety of foods available and prepare to be as flexible as possible. It's frustrating to spend time and effort on a meal only to watch your loved one push their plate away but it isn't your fault or your bad cooking. Your loved one's pickiness is the result of their illness. Don't overly worry yourself regarding what to have for breakfast, lunch, and dinner. Ask nurses, members of the palliative care team, and other caregivers for food suggestions. These folks are a good source of information. Keep in mind that at the very end of your loved one's life, he or she will eat and drink less and less. Feeding him or her will no longer be an issue. At that time, you may find yourself wishing for the fussy days again. I know I did.

Spiritual Considerations

Be mindful of your loved one's spiritual beliefs and respect them if they happen to differ from your own. The peace and comfort of faith plays an important role in easing suffering. For many individuals, cherished beliefs are like a warm, familiar blanket on a cold, blustery day. Supporting your loved one's need to connect with a loving Higher Power is as important as making sure he or she has taken their medication. Forced to contend with an ever-changing body and daily uncertainty, the foundation of your loved one's faith may be the only reliable, trustworthy, and unchanging aspect of their life.

Having said that, it's also quite normal for your loved one's theology to occasionally become a little shaky. Experiencing the emotional ups and downs of a terminal illness can put many a belief system to the test. If your loved one appears troubled, angry, or frightened, ask if he or she would like to speak with a pastoral care worker or a representative of their faith such as a priest, imam or rabbi.

Another way of helping your loved one feel spiritually strengthened is to read stories and prayers from books that have special meaning to them or by putting the radio on a station that has religious programing.

> *Have courage for the great sorrows of life*
> *And patience for the small ones;*
> *And when you have laboriously*
> *Accomplished your daily task,*
> *Go to sleep in peace.*
> *God is awake.*
>
> Victor Hugo

Be a Medical Monitor

One of your responsibilities as a caregiver involves monitoring your loved one's condition. Look for trends such as loss of appetite, increasing nausea, pain, or fatigue. Observe specifics such as whether or not your loved one has a bowel movement each day. If your loved one requires assistance going to the toilet take a peek at their stools while you're in the bathroom with them – are their stools normal in appearance? Is there a change in the consistency or color? Also observe your loved one's urine. Is it getting darker in color? Is there an unusual odor? Keep a record of your observations in a notebook. Inform doctors and nurses of trends or anything else you might notice that's out of the ordinary.

As your loved one's disease progresses, you'll notice their tendency to lie in bed longer. He or she is more likely to lie still and not roll over as often. Their muscles become too weak to reposition themselves. It's during this time of frailty that you'll need to diligently check your loved one for early signs of bed sores. Bedsores can occur on several areas of your loved one's tender skin such as their tailbone, hips, elbows, ankles, and heels. Be sure to discuss this topic with doctors and nurses so that you know exactly what to look for. There are creams available for bed sores as well as anti-bed sore mattresses available for rent. Occupational therapists can also help with this issue.

As a caregiver, you will always be on alert. At night, I slept lightly, listening to the sounds of my grandmother breathing which at times was quite heavy. Hearing her breathe was a relief to me as I knew she was still alive! The next morning, I often teased Nana by telling her she sounded like Darth Vader! I'm not sure what Star Wars character I saw myself as but after a long night I sure didn't look or feel like Princess Leia!

Awkward Situations

Uncomfortable situations may arise during your caregiving journey that will tug upon your heart-strings. Your loved one may need or want certain items that on the surface at least, might not seem a good idea given the time he or she has remaining. Yet, without knowing definitively how long your loved one will live, these moments can result in conflicted feelings for you as a caregiver. Below are a few personal examples of difficult and awkward situations.

One of the saddest occasions for me involved my grandmother asking for a new toaster. The toaster she owned was an ancient silver beast that regularly tossed toast up in the air like a cat playing with a mouse! Most of the time, I failed to catch the flying bread as I was usually multi-tasking rather than waiting for it. The piece of toast (when I found it) was either reduced to something resembling smoldering charcoal or barely browned at all. Most mornings, my grandmother looked forward to toast with jam or banana and she began growing frustrated with the toaster's unpredictability. Several times she asked me to buy her a new one and put the old toaster out of its misery. Expecting Nana to die sooner rather than later, I didn't want to buy a brand-new one. I kept hoping she'd forget about the toaster but she didn't. Returning from shopping excursions, I'd tell her that I forgot to look for one and that I'd remember the next time. Nana probably thought I was becoming senile! Truth be told, I felt badly about the toaster and the sad reminder of Nana's finite time here on earth. If I'd had a crystal ball and knew how much longer my grandmother was going to live, I would have replaced that silly machine on Day One. Unfortunately, none of us can see into the future. All we can do is work with the information we are given and make our best decisions accordingly.

My grandmother also needed a new hearing aid and probably new reading glasses as well. As she was usually too ill to leave the house, I felt the necessary auditory and visual examinations and the adjustments that usually follow would prove too much for her. Again, I believed Nana didn't have much time left. Struggling to hear, she frequently asked me to replace the batteries in her old hearing aid. I doubted doing so made much difference but changed the batteries anyway. Watching Nana sit quietly in her rocking chair, straining to hear and see, I felt a heaviness in my heart that refused to leave me.

You too may be faced with similar situations. Do or say what you feel is best regarding your loved one. Sometimes there's no definitive, cut-and-dry, right or wrong. There's no instruction manual that comes with your loved one's end-of-life care. You're stuck in caregiving quicksand and wish it were otherwise. When your caregiving days are over, you may find yourself second-guessing many of the decisions you made. I did and if that happens for you, then you too will need to make peace with not having had a crystal ball and for being human.

Surprise Your Loved One

Occasionally, surprise the one you're caring for with something fun and unexpected. Our loved ones often pass their days within the confines of a quiet routine. While the familiarity may be comforting to them, there's still room for variety and life's small unforeseen pleasures.

As a younger, healthier person, my grandmother had loved playing ping pong. Coming across a miniature ping pong set in a store, I knew I had to buy it for her. After setting it up on her kitchen table, Nana and I limbered our muscles in anticipation of high-speed volleys and strategic maneuvers! Of course, we ended up playing at turtle speed and Nana soon needed to sit in a chair in order to play. But we laughed and for Nana, it was a break from monotony and thoughts of sickness. It was fun for me too even though I was the person constantly picking the ball up from the floor!

While caregiving, remember that simple things can translate into big smiles for your loved one who likely spends most of their long days in a chair or bed. Find something delightfully unexpected to put a smile on his or her face. They'll appreciate it.

Allow Your Loved One to Exercise Control

For the terminally ill, many aspects of their former lives are relinquished to others. What must it be like to ask someone else to take you to the toilet? To ask someone else for a glass of water? To have someone else dress you? Tuck you into bed? Feed you? Read to you? Cut your nails? Wash you? Giving your loved one the opportunity to retain at least some control over his or her life is a compassionate and important thing to do for them. Even if that control only concerns minor aspects of their lives, it makes an enormous difference to them. Look for ways to give your loved one choice and free-will.

For example, while Nana was a patient in hospital, I regularly took her downstairs to an area where the Ladies Auxiliary sold many lovely hand-made items. A few times, my grandmother asked me to take money from her purse (which was always back home) and buy something that caught her eye. Some of the items she bought didn't make sense such as a pair of pale green baby booties but that didn't matter. The purchase didn't need to make sense to me. It was about Nana being in control. It was about my grandmother using her own money, not mine and buying something she wanted without having to justify it to anyone else. This ties in with the toaster story and the decisions we make as caregivers. It's hard to find balance but do keep in mind the importance, the kindness, of giving your loved one some control over his or her out-of-control life.

Celebrate Important Occasions

Despite your loved one's illness, continue to celebrate and uphold special holidays and other important occasions. Decorate the house, buy special treats, and create precious memories that you'll always treasure. Depending upon the degree to which your loved one's health has deteriorated, engage them as much as possible with the planning unless of course, the occasion is a surprise. These special traditions give meaning to your loved one as well as to yourself. Embrace occasions for the familial closeness they bring.

It's true that holidays and birthdays may be tinged with sadness if the day or season is likely to be the final one that your loved one celebrates. Thinking ahead and visualizing next year's empty chair will fill you with sorrow. Grieving begins early, not after your loved one passes but while he or she is still alive. It's quite alright to feel sad, angry, or whatever else you may feel. Acknowledge these emotions and accept them but also make enough space in your heart to allow peace and healing to enter. Embrace the precious time you and your loved one have together to celebrate meaningful traditions with family and friends.

Knowing my grandmother was about to celebrate her last Christmas, I bought a small artificial tree for her kitchen table and hung a few decorations upon its tiny branches. She loved it! I also hung a few holiday themed pictures upon the walls and even bought a couple of stockings to hang from a countertop. When the decorating was finished, Nana's tiny housing unit looked quite festive. Not only did she enjoy the cheery atmosphere but so did the community nurses and members of the palliative care team who stopped by to check on us. Although sadness was a shadow that followed me that Christmas, I accepted sorrow as normal under the circumstances. At times, I allowed it to have its way with my heart, drenching my face in tears. But each day I also reminded myself to face love's light and enjoy the precious days spent in my grandmother's company.

Use Humor

As mentioned in previous chapters, humor is wonderful medicine. Give a daily dose to you and your loved one. When surrounded by the heaviness of terminal illness, moments of levity make a big difference. A grim countenance doesn't have to go hand-in-hand with end-of-life care. We have control over our attitudes and thoughts even during times of great challenge. Choose to laugh from time to time. It will benefit your loved one and lighten your caregiving days.

Upon my arrival in Australia, I discovered my grandmother could no longer cut her own toenails and was paying a young podiatry assistant to cut her nails once a month at home. I was shocked to find out this woman was charging $80 each visit! That was $8 per toe! I thought that was outrageous especially considering my grandmother's primary source of income was her old-age pension. As the next visit was due, I was quite curious to see what an $80 toenail trim was all about. Was this young lady forced to use a Dremel or power-saw? Was she driving a three-hour round-trip to see Nana? I watched the procedure but couldn't validate an $80 fee for a few snips from a pair of sharp clippers. After the woman left, I decided right then and there that my grandmother wasn't going to dish out another $80. I looked at Nana and told her that I'd cut her nails from now on. I told her, "That's ridiculous paying $80! Why pay $80 when I can cut your nails for $79?!!!" Nana erupted in laughter. I told her I'd gladly give her the family discount; it was the least I could do! We both had many laughs over this as did her nurses when I recounted the story. Of course, I didn't charge Nana anything to cut her nails but sometimes I threatened to whenever she baulked at taking her medicine! Humor is a great way of easing the unpleasantness of dependence and illness.

> *That day is lost on which one has not laughed.*
>
> French Proverb

Practical Tips

1. *Keep Your Loved One in Pajamas*

Eventually, it'll be more comfortable for your loved one to remain in pajamas or a nightgown throughout the day rather than go through the motions of getting completely dressed. You may feel sad knowing the clothes hanging in their closet or folded in their chest of drawers will likely never be worn again. Clothes and other belongings sitting unworn or unused are another reminder of your loved one's journey towards the inevitable.

2. *Keep Important Items in Stock*

Maintain an updated list of essentials so that you'll never run out of important items such as toilet paper or baby wipes. If an item is important, keep one or two extras on hand in case something unforeseen comes up and you can't make it to the store as planned. Don't inconvenience yourself or your loved one. Stay organized to the best of your ability.

3. *Help Your Loved One Write on Cards*

Help your loved one send cards to family and friends on birthdays and other special occasions. Perhaps a family member could purchase a few cards or stamps for you to have on hand. Assist your loved one in writing on the card and addressing the envelope if they need assistance. He or she will appreciate your kindness in helping them continue to connect with those they care about.

Conversation Starters

Don't be afraid to initiate conversations with your loved one even if he or she doesn't bring certain subjects up on their own. Don't assume they don't want to talk about their concerns and emotions. There are many possible reasons why your loved one may not approach you first to discuss their worries. One of them may simply be that he or she doesn't want to upset you. Let your loved one know that they can discuss anything at all with you and that you're strong enough to listen.

What Your Loved One May Want You, Their Caregiver, to Know:

~ I often feel terrible that my illness is disrupting your life. I want it to end quickly for the both of us. I see you getting more tired each day and I know it's because of me. People visit us and say you look awful. I feel guilty because it's my fault. Sometimes you cry and I know it's because of me.

~ Occasionally, you whisper while on the telephone to family and friends. I know you're talking about me. Are you talking about something the doctor said? Is it about when I'm expected to die? Are you saying you wish all of this were over so you can get on with your life?

~ Sometimes I feel depressed. I'm a burden but can't do anything about it. I'm sick of being sick but there's no going back for me. I just want to die but that doesn't mean I no longer love you. Life isn't so great any more. I'm tired, often nauseous, and in varying degrees of pain or discomfort. Moving on to my next adventure is the only way I can feel better again and be more of who I used to be. I want you to understand and accept that.

~ I hate bothering you to help me into the bathroom especially when I know you're worn out or in the middle of doing something else. I wait and wait as long as I can, especially at night, before interrupting you. Sometimes that doesn't work out well and I have an accident which requires even more of your time. I'm left feeling a burden, I never win. I don't know what to do. I feel I'm nothing but a nuisance.

~ I'm so very grateful for your assistance. I'm helpless and can no longer look after myself without you. I'm in your hands and I know that. My vulnerability sometimes reduces me to tears. I know I'm a burden but I also know I need you. I cry in mixed gratitude and frustration.

~ Sometimes you're tired and don't feel like having visitors come over but I enjoy seeing them when I feel up to it. I love you but I need to see other people too. I need my friends. I need their laughter. The little treats and surprises they often bring me are fun. It reminds me of old times and better days. I enjoy hearing their stories. Having visitors gives me a break from my sickness.

~ There's a lot of medication on the table, medical equipment everywhere, and notes and booklets lying around. Nothing is put away. It bothers me to see it all. My house was always so neat and tidy. Now the place is more of a mess. I don't even know where all these items would even go but it sometimes bothers me all the same. Remember this is my home.

~ Sometimes I don't like what you give me to eat. I don't always enjoy the same foods I used to. I don't know why, but some things just don't sit well in my stomach or taste the same anymore. You ask me what I feel like eating and sometimes I really don't know. I can be hungry but not know what I want. I know you feel frustrated but I can't help it.

~ I know I won't get better. I know I need you to look after me. There are many things I can no longer do for myself. But I wish you'd allow me to make some decisions even small ones. Even the tiniest decisions and tiniest tasks that I can do for myself make me feel like a human being again. They give me a sense of worth.

~ I've had a daily routine for years and now the routine is different. Can we keep to my old routine as much as possible? I used to eat at certain times and watch certain television programs that I enjoyed. Could we still maintain some of my old habits? There is comfort in what I know, in the routine I'm used to.

~ Keep me informed as to my medical situation otherwise I become confused about my care, medications, and hospitalizations. So many things are happening to me. Please tell me who the members of the palliative care team are when they visit me and what their job is. Sometimes I forget even though you may have introduced them to me at an earlier time. There are so many people and things to keep track of.

~ I may be sick and not long for this world but there are still things I enjoy doing when I'm having a good day or even a good hour. I enjoy watching old movies even if I fall asleep while watching them. I like music even though my hearing may not be so good. I like playing cards, dominos and computer games. I love sitting out in the sun when it's not too cold or windy. I like watching sports on television. I like it when you read to me or we browse magazines together even though I fall asleep sometimes.

~ Don't be afraid to talk to me about my passing. Sometimes I want to talk about it but I don't want to upset you. Our conversations bring healing and strengthen our relationship. Remember, only my body is dying, not my love for you.

~ Ask me if I want to die at home, in hospice, or hospital if the choice is available. I appreciate this question but I also understand that *where* I die might be different from where I wanted it to be.

~ Sometimes I feel frustrated and upset. I've been living on this earth much longer than you. I know what I'm doing and don't always believe you when I hear you say I'm forgetful and you worry about my safety. I believe I'm still doing things the same way I've always done them.

~ One of the things I most enjoy is telling you stories about my life especially when I was younger. I also love listening to you tell me things about your life experiences too especially funny things that make me laugh.

~ I enjoy the soft touch of a calm pet. There's something comforting about a gentle dog or cat. I like having therapy dogs visit me whenever I'm in hospital.

In closing, as I look back on my caregiving experience, I realize that early on I took over many tasks that my grandmother could still do for herself. I thought she was nearer to death than what she really was. I also thought that 'taking over' was what caregiving was all about. Now, I understand that allowing Nana to do the things she could, while she was able, was a means for her to maintain her sense of independence and dignity a little longer. Be conscious of this with your own loved one. Some of us are Mother hens by nature but giving your special person the opportunity to safely do what they can, while they're able, is important. You'll know when it's time to gently step in.

Chapter 4

Family and Friends

*You have not lived today
Until you have done something
For someone
Who can never repay you.*

John Bunyan

Initially, Nana was embarrassed to be seen sitting in the small fold-up wheelchair the hospital loaned us so that I could take her on short outings. She was especially shy regarding her neighbors. Thus, for the most part, the little wheelchair remained folded and neglected against the wall. One afternoon, Irene, a dear English friend with a cheeky sense of humor came to visit and later upon leaving, suggested I wheel Nana outside to see her off. Unbeknown to my grandmother, Irene's mischievous streak was about to make a sudden appearance. She highjacked the wheelchair and at top speed pushed Nana willy-nilly along the path in front of all her neighbors! Irene laughed and laughed. Clearly, she was having a good time. She zig-zagged with my poor grandmother holding on for dear life and threatened to run over Chee Chee, the neighborhood cat! All I could think of was Nana throwing up from motion-sickness and dying of humiliation! But when the wheelchair slowly turned back in my direction with Irene huffing and puffing, my grandmother was laughing as hard as her friend! Both Nana and Irene had briefly become children again. The spontaneous whimsy had done them both a world of good.

Friends and family members have great potential to bring love and levity to an otherwise sad situation. Their gracious support contributes enormously to the emotional well-being of your loved one and eases your burden as a caregiver by offering hands-on assistance.

Family and Friends Need Time with Their Loved One

Friends and family are deeply affected when a loved one isn't expected to outlive their illness. Knowing the clock is ticking, they desire the opportunity to spend one-on-one time with the person they love. They may wish to share stories, make amends, or create final memories. Spending quality time with their loved one carries special significance for both of them. Unfortunately, while in the midst of caregiving, it can be easy to overlook this. Be as mindful as you can. Hopefully, everyone feels comfortable requesting private time and opportunities for memory-making won't be lost. If you're unsure of the needs of others, please ask them. Remember to also include children who are family members. It's important for them to have a chance to ask questions and gain a better understanding of the situation surrounding their family. Reassure children that they are safe and loved despite the tears of grown-ups.

> *The bitterest tears shed over graves*
> *Are for words left unsaid*
> *And deeds left undone.*
>
> Harriet Beecher Stowe

Allow Family and Friends to Give You a Break

As caregivers, we return refreshed when given respite. Experiencing desperately needed mental spaciousness gives us a physical and psychological boost allowing us to let go and regroup with a sense of peace. An additional benefit is that this rejuvenation positively impacts our loved ones' care.

My aunt sat with my grandmother one day while I attended the Royal Easter Show. The excursion into the world of agriculture was delightful. Walking among merino sheep, cattle, and energetic herding dogs was healing for me. Although avoiding animal droppings proved somewhat challenging for my shoes! The earthy mixture of aromas smelled wonderful compared to the sterile odors of hand-sanitizer, anti-rash cream, and baby wipes back at Nana's house! My aunt received a Show Bag as gratitude for a wonderful day of restoration.

Friendship doubles joy
And cuts grief in half.

Francis Bacon

Family and Friends are 'One of Many'

At times, family and friends may innocently overwhelm you with their well-meaning actions by forgetting that they are one of a group of people endeavoring to help or seek information. While being inundated with good-intentions may not sound too bad, the cumulative effect can be surprisingly stressful. This is especially true as your loved one's condition deteriorates and you become more fatigued as their caregiver.

Respectful communication, education, and awareness are key factors in smoothing potential problems with those wanting to help you and your loved one. It's important for each family member and friend to appreciate that although they are loved, they are also *one of many*. For example, they are:

- One of many calling on the telephone.
- One of many emailing.
- One of many knocking unannounced at the door.
- One of many wanting to visit.
- One of many dropping off food.
- One of many you will contact when your loved one has passed away.

While close-knit family and friends are usually considerate and work well together towards a common goal, we all know individuals who are regrettably, the opposite. With few boundaries, these folks can be a nuisance. You may need to ask these individuals to pace themselves in regards to certain activities involving you and your loved one. Good luck with these folks; be strong and put your foot down!

Communicating clearly and shining a spotlight upon potential issues will benefit you going forward. Gingerly walking on eggshells and hoping certain individuals won't misunderstand or feel hurt is unpleasant. Remember, you're not responsible for the thoughts and feelings of others – they are. You're simply trying to be a caregiver for a terminally ill person. That's a pretty tough job and you don't need additional anxiety thrown into the mix.

Concerns Regarding Food and Beverages

Feeding a terminally ill person is often difficult under the best of circumstances. Matters can become further complicated if family members disagree about the food and beverages your loved one should be given. Some individuals feel strongly about nutrition while others believe it's kinder to let your loved one eat or drink whatever they'd like. Be prepared for comments that run the spectrum and remember, most concerns come from a place of caring. Discuss the consumption of alcohol in particular, as well as food with your loved one's doctor and then share the information with family and friends.

Relationship Issues

Relationship issues easily become magnified during times of stress. Most of us will admit to having one or two challenging family members or friends – those who push our buttons and easily get under our skin. We love them one minute then entertain thoughts of choking them the next! Unfortunately, the nature of caregiving typically doesn't lend itself to having the time or energy to deal with these individuals. Overworked and stressed, you cannot take on the additional roles of traffic officer and therapist! Speak honestly and firmly with troublesome individuals but remember, difficult people are typically poor listeners. You may need to engage in repeated conversations with them in order to get your message across.

Each of us has a different set of communication skills and life experiences even within the same family. Misunderstandings, fear-based assumptions, and concerns are common in emotionally charged situations. Terminal illness is unasked for, inconvenient, disruptive, and life-changing. The devastating disease affecting your loved one is beyond anyone's control. We cannot save the one we love. As reality hits, sorrow and anger may alternate and wash over us like an emotional storm surge. Each family member and friend will react uniquely to the inevitable loss of their loved one. Each one of us is struck down and the question becomes – how can we lift one another up in a kind and supportive manner? How can we grow in patience and compassion as emotions run grief's gauntlet? We must find common ground and build upon it. Typically, our collective bedrock is the love and affinity we share for the special person at the center of the storm, the one who is unwell. Let this be a time of coming together rather than drawing apart.

When Family and Friends Choose Not to Visit

Sometimes, a family member or friend may feel uncomfortable visiting their loved one. Some choose not to visit at all. Perhaps their loved one's disease crystalizes their own fears of illness and mortality. They aren't ready to see themselves reflected through their loved one's vulnerability. Some may prefer to remember their loved one as they once were prior to the illness rather than seeing them as they are now. Be prepared for this scenario in case your loved one mentions a specific family member or friend by name and wonders why he or she hasn't come to visit.

Not surprisingly, many family members and friends are upset by their loved one's appearance and loss of function. Weight loss in the terminally ill can be dramatic especially if the person visiting hasn't seen him or her for some time. An upset or shocked visitor may not stay long. Witnessing a once strong and vibrant person being spoon fed or needing undergarments changed can be a huge shock. Prepare family and friends ahead of time regarding your loved one's current physical, emotional, and mental condition if they haven't seen him or her recently. As a caregiver involved with your loved one's daily care, it's easy to forget how different they must appear to others who see them infrequently.

Occasionally, friends and family may not know what to talk about when visiting their loved one. They dread an uncomfortable silence once they've finished discussing the weather. Death is the elephant in the room. In Western culture in particular, we are raised to avoid this particular pachyderm rather than acknowledge its presence. Cultivating acceptance of death as well as other aspects of life that are beyond our control can be challenging. Letting go of our fear requires courage and conscious contemplation of sickness and death. Only then, will we find the fragrant rose among the thorns.

It's sad whenever a friend or family member chooses not to visit your loved one, who may have been looking forward to seeing them. Our loved ones, whether at home or in the hospital, dearly need the love and support of others. But some individuals are simply not emotionally able to face illness or death. Give these people a little love, understanding, and patience. Perhaps they will try to visit again, on a day in which they feel stronger. In my grandmother's case, two family members (who I knew loved her) visited and afterwards told me they wouldn't come back again as it was too upsetting. Later however, they had a change of heart and returned. I was proud of them for facing their demons and Nana was overjoyed at seeing them once more.

> *If someone is facing a difficult time,*
> *One of the kindest things*
> *You can do for them is to say,*
> *"I'm just going to love you through this."*
>
> Molly Freidenfeld

Caregiving Skills – Helpful Critique or Criticism?

Uncle Fred, Aunt Dolorous, or cousin Bill may have their own opinions regarding the care of your loved one. This is normal. You'd have your own thoughts too if circumstances were reversed. Because you care, you'd look for ways in which certain tasks could be done better or more efficiently, especially if you knew the caregiver was struggling in his or her role. Listen to family and friends as many of their suggestions may be helpful to you and always appreciate opinions that are stated with respect. If you're fortunate, one of them may have been a caregiver themselves and have much wisdom to impart to you.

Depending upon family dynamics however, there may be times during which little you do as a caregiver will be looked upon favorably. That's life plain and simple. Many caregivers experience these issues with a particular relative. Should you find your caregiving skills unkindly criticized, remind yourself that you're doing the best you can in a highly imperfect and ever-changing environment. Don't be too hard on yourself just because someone else is. Mentally separate yourself from rudeness and disrespect. Unkind words speak volumes about the person saying them, not you. Rise above it. Eagles fly higher to free themselves from smaller birds who annoyingly nip their tail feathers. Be an eagle.

Chat, Laugh, and Enjoy

No matter who we are, we all need something upbeat to look forward to. Creating opportunities for friends and family to come together for a little fun, benefits everyone. Perhaps a brainstorming session over lunch might facilitate a few ideas such as board games or classic movies. Of course, your loved one's current physical and mental condition will dictate the activity and amount of time spent doing it but enjoying one another's company needn't be complicated.

For example, each Wednesday afternoon our friends Betty and Irene came over after lunch and the four of us huddled around Nana's kitchen table playing a card game called Five Crowns. We'd drink tea and nibble from a bowl of candy or a plate of biscuits. Occasionally, there were friendly food fights involving popcorn especially between my grandmother and I! Nana loved Wednesdays! She looked forward to the tasty snacks and laughter. Catching up on her friend's weekly news and silly stories took Nana's mind off more unpleasant things. It was a much-needed break from her illness and I enjoyed it too. Moments of levity spent with those we love can really make a difference in light of the serious side of being unwell.

Always laugh when you can.
It's cheap medicine.

Lord Byron

Managing Telephone Calls

Explain to family and friends the importance of keeping telephone calls relatively short, especially as your loved one's disease progresses. Without employing a professional secretary, answering numerous daily phone calls can quickly become unmanageable especially if you're the only person answering the telephone.

One possible solution to the issue of communicating with multiple people is to find one or two individuals willing to be co-distributers of information. This is ideal if you're the sole caregiver. Of course, not everyone likes getting second-hand information. Some prefer to hear updates straight from the horse's mouth, so to speak. That's understandable but if you're struggling with time constraints and stress, having an additional person assist in passing along updates is a viable option.

To illustrate the need to manage telephone calls, there were days during which Nana's phone would ring off the hook! Unfortunately, she had no answering machine or service. Family and friends continuously called at all hours, not realizing they were *one of many* doing so and not realizing I was terribly tired. In addition to phone calls from family and friends, I was also receiving calls from community nurses and members of the palliative care team. Speaking with them however, was an entirely different matter and these individuals limited their time on the telephone.

As Nana's condition deteriorated, everyone but the dog called more frequently. I'm not sure why the dog didn't join in but I do thank him! With cumulative phone calls and neighbors knocking on the front door, my blood pressure shot through the roof! At times, I contemplated quitting my caregiving job for an easier one such as Air Traffic Controller at Heathrow Airport! While the phone rang and the door was pounded upon, my grandmother had needs: toileting, accidents cleaned up, given medications, dressed or undressed, helped into bed, hair washed, meals cooked and fed. All of these tasks take time when involving someone who is frail and very unwell. Many non-caregivers fail to realize that looking after someone who is physically weak involves slow-motion movements. Nothing is done quickly.

At times, I also found it difficult to end telephone conversations despite repeatedly pleading, "I'm sorry but I need to go now." Some folks are simply chatty. I didn't want to be rude and hang up. I loved these people but the leisurely conversations of my pre-caregiving days were long gone. These were different times now. There was an occasion in which Nana had an accident when I wasn't off the phone in time to take her to the toilet. The person on the telephone wasn't the one to clean up the mess – I was. They weren't the one feeling embarrassed – my grandmother was. But I take responsibility for that. I needed to hang up and let possible hurt feelings take care of themselves.

Lend Your Ear

One of the best ways family and friends can help you as a caregiver, is by offering to listen whenever you need to share your feelings and concerns. Caregiving is challenging on many levels and you'll need to talk about the ways it's affecting you. For family and friends however, listening may not come easy. What you're saying directly involves the one they love and often the conversation quickly reverts back to that person. Perhaps they feel you'll have plenty of time to talk in the future once their loved one has died. To be heard in the present, you may need to emphasize just how much you need their ears.

Your experiences and feelings as a caregiver deserve to be acknowledged. You need emotional support. If you're unable to find a trusted friend or family member to share your feelings with, seek out professional listeners such as members of the palliative care team, counsellors, or members of one's spiritual community. Don't keep your emotions bottled up inside you.

Food Storage Issues

On several occasions, my grandmother and I had more visitors than usual within a particular week. With good intentions, each person happened to bring food for our future meals. We must have looked skinny! What thoughtful gestures! Unfortunately, by the end of the week there were enough casseroles, soups, and stew to feed the entire Jamaican Bobsled Team, the London Choir, and the citizens of Botswana! With Nana's miniscule refrigerator and freezer, it quickly became impossible for us to keep all the food we were given. You may need to mention food storage issues (if you have them) to generous family and friends prior to their visits or otherwise prepare to buy a bigger freezer!

Conversation Starters

Feel free to have a friend photocopy the conversation starters below or perhaps the entire chapter to hand out among family and friends. Your caregiving experience can be buoyed by others or inadvertently made more difficult. In a nutshell, the most important thing for each person to understand is that they are *one of many*. Bringing a greater awareness of this to others will help immensely as you walk your loved one Home.

What I, as Caregiver, Would Like My Family and Friends to Know:

~ It's important for you to know ahead of time that my needs as a caregiver will change as our loved one's disease progresses. What I need now, I may not need later.

~ Please ask *how* you can help me rather than make assumptions as to what's needed. Although having said that, there may be times in which I'm so tired and overwhelmed that I don't know how you can assist me unless you have a magic wand!

Some questions you might ask me include:

- Can I take you to the supermarket or go for you?
- Can I cook or bring a meal? What can our loved one eat?
- Can I do a load of washing or ironing?
- Can I sit with our loved one so you can take a nap, go out for a break, or get a haircut?
- Can I help with yard work or clean house?
- Can I make tea or coffee for everyone during get-togethers?
- Can I wash the dishes for you following a get-together?
- Would you like company or need transportation to a doctor's appointment?
- Would our loved one like a donation of old magazines to browse or DVDs to watch?
- Can I pick up medication or disposable underwear from the pharmacist for you?
- Do you need petrol in the car?
- Would you like your shoulders massaged? Always answer 'yes' to this question!

Some suggestions for brightening our loved one's day include:

- Read to him or her.
- Sing much loved songs together.
- Work on a puzzle or coloring book.
- Play cards or board games.
- Reminisce. Tell stories or browse photo albums.
- Give him or her gentle arm, leg, or foot massages.
- Watch a movie or television program together.
- If our loved one is mobile and feeling well enough, take him or her to a coffee shop, store, or garden area.

~ Please don't worry if you're physically unable to help. You can always offer a prayer. Prayers bring comfort during difficult times and are greatly appreciated. You can also offer to listen whenever our loved one or myself need someone to talk to.

~ When visiting, please ask ahead of time what type of food to bring. Our loved one's ability to tolerate or enjoy certain foods changes frequently. She or he may no longer enjoy or tolerate food they once loved. Often, I end up with a refrigerator full of food that our loved one can't eat. Also, as our loved one grows weaker, choking while eating or drinking can become an issue. Asking ahead of time gives me the opportunity to explain that soup or something pureed might be best rather than arriving with hamburgers! In addition, washing large bowls, plates, and casserole containers afterward overwhelms me as I'm so dreadfully tired. In addition, I have to find a place to store these items until you return. Storage space is at a premium. Remember, you are *one of many* family and friends who well-meaningly drop off food.

~ Please remember you're not the only person calling me on the telephone on any given day. Unfortunately, I'm unable to have long conversations. Your calls are truly appreciated and you're loved, but at times I'm inundated with phone calls and requests for visits. This exacerbates my bone-weariness and stress as I burn the candle at both ends. As our loved one deteriorates, more of my time is required in caring for him or her around the clock. Keeping phone calls relatively short is immensely helpful.

~ Please keep visits short-lived when our loved one's condition worsens. He or she has a terminal illness and tires easily. Often, our loved one attempts to hold themselves together because you're visiting, only to collapse in a heap immediately after you leave. In addition, as a caregiver, I'm worn out with unending tasks and I too often wish to collapse in a heap after you leave but unlike our loved one, I can't. If our loved one is doing well during your visit, we may ask you to stay longer.

~ Sometimes our loved one overhears you tell me that I look tired. Perhaps he or she believes it's their fault that I'm worn out. Just in case, please protect our loved one by voicing concerns regarding my appearance privately.

~ Avoid appearing at the front door unannounced. Please call first. With so much involved in caring for our loved one, knocking on the door unannounced can really throw a wrench into the bicycle wheel. I've been in the bathroom trying to clean Nana while someone continuously pounded on the front door calling our names. Nana's heart and mine were racing as several times I shouted back, "Just a minute!" So please, call on the phone first. It's the respectful thing to do.

~ If you have a day and time planned in which to visit, be aware that the situation with our loved one can change quickly. Prepare to be flexible should that happen.

~ Mornings are a particularly busy time of day for caregivers. Please don't phone during the first half of the morning. It's preferable to ask, "When is best time to call you?" Quite honestly, there's never a truly good time as each day brings its own unique challenges and unexpected situations. But there's always a lot of activity in the mornings involving taking our loved one to the toilet, washing them, giving medications, making breakfast, giving more medications, taking them to the toilet again, dressing them, straightening their bed, and changing sheets as necessary, washing soiled nightclothes, community nurses stopping by, and so forth. These tasks take much longer than most people realize when caring for someone who is weak and unwell. In addition, phoning too early in the morning can wake up our loved one who may still be asleep.

~ Please understand that I'm not always able to return your telephone calls or emails as promptly as you might like. It's nothing personal. I'm occupied and worn out. Please avoid peppering me with calls and emails asking why I haven't returned your call yet or been in touch with you recently. That only adds to the pressure I'm under. The fact that you haven't heard from me in a timely manner, speaks volumes in and of itself. Remember, you are *one of many*. Your patience and understanding are appreciated.

~ Please avoid calling on the telephone later than _____ (fill in the blank) at night. It takes time to settle a terminally ill person comfortably into bed. Also, my fatigue is enormous by the end of the day and I may possibly have only a small window of time to myself before dropping like a log onto my own mattress. Often, I'm awoken repeatedly during the night to see to the needs of our loved one and am desperate for a quiet moment in which to unwind. Furthermore, calling later than _____ (fill in the blank) may wake our loved one who hears the telephone ringing. This happened with my grandmother. Whenever Nana woke up, she needed to use the bathroom and couldn't do so on her own. Also, being woken up seemed to trigger her awareness of physical discomfort/pain and she often needed additional pain medication.

~ Should you decide to stay with our loved one for a few hours and give me a much-needed break, make sure you're given all pertinent phone numbers: hospital, doctor, or community nurse. Make sure you understand our loved one's medications - know when and how they are given. Know what time our special person usually eats and what they might enjoy. Are there toileting issues? Do you know where cleaning products are kept should an accident occur? Know the whereabouts of clean underwear, pads, baby wipes, other cleaning products, nightgowns & pajamas, and clean bedsheets. Are there mobility issues? Do you understand and recognize the signs of what might constitute a medical emergency? Is there a Do Not Resuscitate order (DNR) and where is it kept? These are some of the things you may need to be aware of should you offer to stay with our loved one while I'm away. Taking on this responsibility for a few hours is greatly appreciated.

~ I'm grateful for any suggestions in regards to better care for our loved one but please refrain from criticism. It's normal to walk into our loved one's home and feel there are things you would do differently if you were the person caring for them. By all means offer helpful suggestions especially if you have any caregiving experience or knowledge. But avoid being unkind.

~ Please feel free to send encouraging or amusing cards in the mail just for fun. Your love and support help me immensely as I try to cope with stress, sadness, and working long hours with little sleep. While caring for my grandmother I often received cards for no reason at all. They really made my day.

~ When our dear one finally passes, there'll be many telephone calls and emails I'll need to make to family and friends. Now is not the time to nit-pick over who was called first, second, or third as though the order of phone calls signifies the order of one's importance. The order of calls telling of our loved one's passing is nothing personal. Please don't make it so. Now is the time to support one another in shared grief and healing.

Sometimes the person who has been here
For everyone else
Needs someone to be there for them.

Author Unknown

Chapter Five

The Palliative Care Team and Other Supporters

If I can stop one heart from breaking,
I shall not live in vain;
If I can ease one life the aching,
Or cool one pain,
Or help one fainting robin
Unto his nest again,
I shall not live in vain.

Emily Dickinson

Nana was too unwell to leave the house to buy me a Christmas card on what would be her final Christmas. Knowing this, a thoughtful community nurse took the time to hand-make a card on Nana's behalf so that my grandmother had something to give to me. To this day I treasure that card. This lovely nurse didn't have to do that. It wasn't part of her job description. But she chose to go the extra mile and do something special. I was often deeply touched by the kindness of those working to assist my grandmother (and myself) on her end-of-life journey. You too, will feel the same way about your support staff.

Aside from the involvement of a palliative care team, many others including pharmacists, paramedics, and those offering community-based services will aid you as you steer your caregiving ship through unfamiliar waters. These dedicated individuals will be your main source of information and support. Should you feel you're drowning in a sea of tasks and swirling emotions, these are the people who will toss you a life-preserver.

Education and Communication

Upon your caregiving adventure, unexpected situations will arise and you'll need to know who to turn to and what to expect as your loved one's condition deteriorates. Minimize being blind-sided by asking questions of the professionals around you. Educate yourself about your loved one's illness, palliative care, available resources, and the dying process. Being informed will help you make better decisions.

Communicate honestly with community and hospital-based staff regarding your loved one and yourself. When they ask, "How are you doing?" resist the temptation to say you're managing when clearly, you're not. This journey is not only about your loved one. It's about you too. You matter. If you don't take care of yourself, you won't be able to take care of your loved. It's that simple.

Early into caregiving and thoroughly overwhelmed, I distinctly remember the moment in which a lovely Irish nurse took me aside after examining Nana and asked, "And how are *you* doing?" Up to that point, no-one had asked how I was doing. I recall pausing for a brief moment before bursting into tears. I suppose my tears were the unspoken answer to her question! The much-needed conversation that followed really helped me. A huge weight had been lifted from my shoulders that day. I had been keeping my emotions inside and now had shared something of myself with another person. My secret was out – I was struggling in my caregiving role.

Following that day, everyone wearing a badge or uniform wanted to know how I was doing. It meant so much to know there was a safety-net of people ready to catch me should I falter. More importantly, it meant my grandmother would be taken care of if that were to happen. Neither she nor I were going to crash-land.

Community Nursing Services

Your loved one may require regular medical care at home using a community-based service. This care may be necessary daily, every few days, or weekly according to doctor recommendations and end-of-life management plans. Depending upon the country or state in which your loved one resides, he or she may receive government assistance in paying for these services.

In addition to the palliative care team at Nana's hospital, she used a community service known as Nurses on Wheels and no, the nurses weren't on roller-skates! Initially, these nurses drove to Nana's home twice a day to apply morphine gel directly to a portion of her colorectal tumor. Aside from their nursing duties, Nana and I enjoyed their friendly visits. As a new caregiver, these nurses were also an excellent source of information and encouragement.

Being elderly *and* on pain medications meant bouts of constipation were a frequent issue for my grandmother. Complications due to constipation can have serious consequences so community nurses (who drew the short straw) took turns giving Nana regular enemas. Over the ensuing hours that followed, these enemas were the gift that kept on giving! Nana's tiny housing unit quickly turned into the NASA Jet Propulsion Laboratory! From supermarket shelves, I bought a variety of aerosol spray cans promising me a Summer Breeze, Coastal Linen, or Field of Roses. None quite delivered what they advertised! Later, as Nana's disease progressed, nurses thankfully stopped giving her enemas. At this point, they only came to periodically change the fentanyl patch on her chest.

Towards the very end of Nana's life, nurses simply popped in for a quick, "Hello" to make sure my grandmother and I were doing alright. Often, if there was an issue, they contacted the hospital on our behalf. Knowing these wonderful nurses were active throughout our area and readily available by mobile phone was comforting.

Our greatest strength
Lies in the gentleness and tenderness
Of our heart.

Rumi

Maintain Good Relationships

Foster positive relationships with the professionals who assist you and your loved one. These individuals work hard on your behalf and really do care. Their jobs aren't easy as they work within the challenging confines surrounding death, dying, and family issues. Surely this must wear on them at times. Please keep this in mind and express gratitude for all they do. When working with the general public, one sees both the best and the worst in people. Be one of the better ones.

What is Palliative Care?

Palliative care is a rapidly growing component of modern medicine whose focus is to provide specialized care for children and adults with serious or life-threatening illness. Alleviating suffering and improving the quality of life for patients and their families is their primary goal. As you can imagine, the field of palliative care is multi-faceted, requiring a diverse group of people including doctors, nurses, social workers, pastoral care, occupational therapists, speech therapists, and volunteers.

Members of Your Loved One's Team

Doctors and Nurses

In the trenches doing the front-line medical work, doctors and nurses will be your go-to for medication, symptom management, and specific information regarding your loved one's illness. Don't be afraid to ask questions any time you don't fully understand your loved one's medications, changing symptoms, or comfort care. You can also ask them what the dying process will look like and what to do if your loved one dies at home.

Social Workers

Assisting patients and families navigate the uncertainties, nuances, and management of end-of-life care are the social workers. They offer helpful advice and information on a number of fronts including nursing home placement, community services, family issues, and eligibility for financial assistance. Listen to their recommendations with an open mind and read any literature they give you. Being aware of all available options in caring for your loved one is important. You never know how your situation may change in the future.

    Feel free to speak openly and honestly with your social worker regarding any concerns you may have. You'll find him or her to be a non-judgmental and patient listener. Allow yourself to be supported in making wise decisions.

Be brave enough to start
A conversation that matters.

Dau Voir

Occupational Therapists

Occupational therapists (OTs) identify your loved one's current physical abilities and support them as necessary. Engaging in the activities of daily life is important for your loved one. As his or her abilities gradually deteriorate, OT's will recommend necessary adjustments. This typically involves the use of specialized equipment which they will teach you and your loved one how to safely use.

Occupational therapists can also demonstrate the most effective and safe ways to 'shift' your loved one from Point A to Point B, such as chair to bed, in order to minimize caregiver back strain. As your loved one's muscles grow weaker, he or she will become heavier for you to physically manage. OTs can help you with any hands-on functional issues you may have.

Pastoral Care

Pastoral care workers provide compassionate emotional and spiritual support to patients and their families. Their active listening skills, encouragement, and understanding are of great benefit when facing terminal illness.

My grandmother and I were fortunate to have a wonderful pastoral care person who took us under her wing. She called frequently on the telephone to inquire how we were and also scheduled regular in-home visits.

Volunteers

Throughout Nana's illness, I met volunteers of all ages and backgrounds who either worked in the local community or in her hospital. All were hard-working and dedicated. Many of them knew first-hand what it was to be a caregiver or lose a loved one. You'll meet them too and like me, marvel at their professionalism and capacity for kind-heartedness.

Paramedics

Your loved one may periodically require paramedics to come to the home, evaluate his or her current medical status, and transport them to the hospital. Their appearance at your home will bring enormous relief as these highly skilled individuals see to the needs of your loved one. Paramedics will require a list of your loved one's medications and a DNR order if you have one so have these readily available.

The Night the Cavalry Came

The last few hours my grandmother spent inside the tiny home she loved weren't pleasant. In the early hours of a chilly morning, I was awoken by Nana ringing her bedside bell and calling my name. Previously, she'd been unable to lift her upper practical tips
body and swing her legs over the side of the bed without my assistance so I was shocked to find her in the darkened bedroom having done just that. I knew something was wrong. Turning on the bedroom light, I could see Nana trembling all over. At first, I thought she was simply very cold. Looking back on it now, I suspect she may have been having seizures.

Nana urgently needed to use the toilet and was extremely unsteady as I guided her hands to the handlebars of her walker and into the bathroom. Once there, I could barely position her near the toilet seat due to her shaking. Although Nana was speaking, her voice trembled and I had trouble understanding her. I wasn't even sure if she was making sense. Suddenly, she lost all bladder and bowel control while becoming severely nauseous. Unfortunately, my grandmother wasn't positioned properly on the toilet and her legs had buckled. The bathroom was a terrible mess of stools, urine, and blood. It was everywhere and on everything. I felt sickened by it but could do nothing.

Nana was dry-retching as I held her upper body over the sink. Enormously overwhelmed and desperately needing help, the stark realization that I was alone struck me hard. An awful feeling of dread, isolation, and responsibility dropped like rocks onto my shoulders. My heart pounded and I felt shaky. I wanted to scream, "I can't do this," but nothing came out of my mouth. Struggling, I awkwardly placed Nana upon the small seat attached to her walker. Holding her torso with one arm so she wouldn't fall off, I dragged her and the walker backward and back into her bedroom. Nana was like a rag doll. It was difficult moving her on my own. There was a trail of blood and liquid stools on the floor behind us.

Maneuvering Nana as close to her bed as I could, I lifted her onto it and straightened her small body, covering her with blankets. Nana's clothes and body were so extensively soiled that I didn't know where to begin when I thought of cleaning her. Ideally, she needed to be showered but she was too weak for me to safely hold and wash by myself, not to mention the bathroom floor was a disaster that we'd be stepping in!

After several minutes of lying in bed, Nana seemed to improve. She was no longer trembling, no longer nauseous, and could speak clearly. But she was lying in her own filth and that upset me. I couldn't give her a kiss without stepping in the mess on the carpet by the bed. Her little slippers were so dirty they'd need to be thrown away. I was heartsick. My dear grandmother!

It was obvious Nana had experienced some kind of medical event and equally obvious that I could no longer care for her immediate needs by myself. She was my beloved grandmother and deserved a level of care that I could no longer provide. I felt helpless. We were both falling off the side of the mountain and I needed to grab onto a rope quickly before it was too late.

I told Nana I'd have to call the hospital and have her admitted. She had only been home from the previous admission a short while and understandably didn't want to return again so soon. She cried, asking me not to take her there. She wanted to stay home. I don't think Nana fully understood all that had happened. Watching her weep and hearing her quiet voice plead with me while lying in all that mess was emotionally distressing. Utterly heart-broken, I apologized to my grandmother for my inability to do more. But I needed help. I wasn't wearing a superhero cape that morning and probably never was. Perhaps, my kryptonite as a caregiver had been thinking I could do the impossible until the impossible presented itself.

Soon, three young paramedics arrived at the house – two men and one woman. I described the events that had occurred and recounted Nana's medical history and vast collection of medications. They took Nana's vital signs. None of which were normal. She softly asked them whether she was going to die. You could have heard a pin-drop! I broke the uncomfortable silence by telling Nana that doctors at the hospital would stabilize her and probably readjust her medications. In truth, I knew none of this looked good for her. My dear grandmother would pass away in hospital eleven days later.

Paramedics spoke with Nana in such a tender manner, it was as if she were their own grandmother. Their kindness towards her helped calm me. They decided to clean her prior to transporting her to hospital. Lifting her out of bed, the two male paramedics each held Nana by the arm and shoulder trying to help her stand. She was terribly weak so they held the majority of her body weight. Respectfully, the young men looked away while the female paramedic removed Nana's soiled nightgown. The upsetting sight of seeing my 95-year-old grandmother (a normally clean, well-groomed lady) standing naked shivering in the cold while baby wipes were used to remove feces and blood from her back, bottom, legs, and feet has haunted me ever since.

Thankfully, those paramedics interjected as much dignity and kindness as they could in both word and deed. They were the cavalry who came to the rescue. Later, Nana never spoke of the episode and I wondered whether she even remembered what had happened during those chilly early morning hours. For me, time has slowly healed the intrusive flashbacks although I will always carry the memories of that sad incident.

While walking your loved one Home, you'll meet many fine people along the way just as I did. They'll touch you with their professionalism and benevolence. They are your safety-net while on the flying trapeze that is caregiving.

Kindness is just love with its work boots on.

Author Unknown

Conversation Starters

Below, are a few suggestions for possible conversations you may wish to have with members of the palliative care team.

What You as a Caregiver Would Like the Palliative Care Team to Know:

~ Aside from myself, you're the guardians of my loved one's vulnerability. You educate, encourage, comfort, and problem solve. I'm grateful for all you do.

~ Please help me chisel away the 'granite' encasing my brain. Sleep-deprived and overwhelmed, good judgement and sound decision-making are sometimes difficult for me. Over time, I've morphed into a heavily harnessed horse wearing blinders. I make the motions, pulling the weighty carriage of my loved one and their illness. Your patience with my sluggish struggle is appreciated.

~ Don't give up on me when I appear not to listen, brush you off, or feel I know best. It's during these times that I most need assistance in steering my caregiving ship clear of icebergs. I'm adrift upon uncharted waters, unfamiliar with the perils of the ocean I must traverse. Deep down, I know you are a safe haven upon which I can rely.

~ Honestly, I didn't realize I could talk about myself and my needs as a caregiver until you asked me how I was doing. Initially, I believed the work you did was *only* about my loved one. Thank you for listening and giving me a forum. You understand what I'm going through in ways that others don't.

~ I want you to know I'm afraid. When you're not physically with me in my home, my loved one's life is in my hands and my hands are shaking.

~ Thank you for offering kind suggestions for doing a task more efficiently. I also appreciate the information you give me regarding the many programs that are available to assist my loved one and myself. Caregiving is new for me. I'm completely reliant upon the information you share.

~ There are times I wish to speak with you privately but am unable to do so because my loved one is either in the room when you visit or in the same room as the telephone when you call me. I'm not always able to be forthcoming in answering your questions due to this lack of privacy.

~ Please explain to those of us who are new to caregiving and palliative care that the hospital is different from a nursing home and cannot indefinitely keep a stabilized patient even though they are slowly dying. Sometimes the distinction is blurry.

~ I often wonder what dying will be like for my loved one. What will he or she be aware of and experience? Will he or she be afraid? Will it hurt? What I don't know and don't understand, frightens me.

~ Thank you for being honest even when honesty isn't easy for me to hear.

~ There's a reason I often turn down offers for respite. Many community services only offer short respite periods and I'm reliant upon public transportation. No sooner have I arrived somewhere and it's almost time for me to turn around and come back. I'd be spending my short respite looking at my watch, stressed about possibly missing the return bus. I'm not turning down respite because I don't want it but unfortunately, there just isn't enough time for short-term respite periods to work for me without a car.

~ My loved one often resists using assistive equipment, especially at first. Each new piece of equipment marks a point of no return for him or her. "I'll never be able to walk on my own again if I start using a cane" or "What will others think if they see me using a cane?" Later, following more deterioration, he or she may progress to a walker or wheelchair. Each new piece of equipment marks a loss of function, a step further from independence yet also allows him or her to remain self-mobile. Assistive equipment is sometimes seen as a sign of weakness by my loved one, something "old people" use. To him or her, devices seem to represent being another step closer to the end of life's journey.

~ Thank you for patiently answering my endless questions and for telling me what to expect as my loved one's condition deteriorates so that I'm not blind-sided.

~ I have no prior experience with either palliative care or caring for a terminally ill family member. Instead, I have a family history of loved ones dying unexpectedly and quickly. The situation I find myself in as my loved one slowly dies from a progressive illness is new and frightening. Because of that, I may require more education from you on a variety of fronts.

What You May Like the Palliative Care Team to Know About Nursing Home Discussions:

~ Discussing a possible nursing home admission is difficult for me to engage in. I realize you mean well and are thinking of what's best for my loved one and myself but inwardly I cringe whenever the subject is brought up. I'm scared and want you to know that.

~ I fear the stress and sadness my loved one may experience if he or she leaves the familiar surroundings of their own home, especially while so unwell. Won't this stress hasten their passing?

~ It's a self-centered thought but I fear a nursing home admission means I've failed as a caregiver and I've let my loved one down.

~ Emotionally, it feels as though my loved one will be taken away from me if they enter a nursing home. We'll be separated in some sense and I'll no longer see as much of him or her as I once did when we were home together around the clock.

~ As my loved one's caregiver, I tend to feel no-one else can give my loved one what I can give them. I know him or her best and have a long history with them while nursing home staff do not. They may make a mistake or become impatient with my loved one. This is something that worries me. I need help in resolving this concern in order to move forward with discussions. I need help letting go.

~ There's a part of me that knows everything would work out if my loved one were in a nursing home. But taking the initial steps and making the actual move feels heart-wrenching. I don't know if I can bare seeing my loved one upset during the transfer and settling in period. I want to bury my head in the sand and have someone else do the unpleasant work of taking my loved one there and making them comfortable. Then I can lift up my head, shake off the sand, and with fingers crossed, hope for the best. I don't want to be the 'bad guy' in my loved one's end-of-life story.

Chapter 6

Hospital Admissions: Practice Drills for the End

You cannot do a kindness too soon,
For you never know
How soon
It will be too late.

Ralph Waldo Emerson

My grandmother was admitted into hospital on numerous occasions while I was caring for her. For both of us, the string of admissions were a rollercoaster ride of emotions. Some of these hospitalizations were frightening as I wondered whether Nana's passing was at hand. I saw other families and their loved ones going through similar circumstances. While many patients received care and returned to their homes, some did not. Too often, I witnessed the immediate aftermath of families losing their loved one. Seeing and hearing their deepest cries of sorrow crushed me. Looking at them, I saw myself, knowing one day it would be my turn.

A Mixing Bowl of Emotions

On your caregiving journey, you may accompany your loved one through multiple hospitalizations or very few. These admissions may trigger a variety of emotions. If you're new to caregiving, it's also possible that your loved one's first admission with you at the helm of the caregiving ship may produce a few self-doubts. For example, during my grandmother's first hospitalization, I questioned my abilities as a caregiver. Was it my fault she was admitted? Could I have done something differently that would have prevented her hospitalization? Was I feeding her well? When medicating her for breakthrough pain or nausea, was I doing it correctly? At the time, I wasn't sufficiently aware of the many ways the need for hospitalization could present itself. Should you have similar thoughts when your loved one goes into hospital, please know you aren't alone in having them. Remember, your loved one's illness is placing them in hospital and not you. Your goal as a caregiver is *not* to keep your loved one out of hospital. He or she is succumbing to their disease. Hospitalizations stabilize your loved one along the way, ensuring that their worsening symptoms such as pain and nausea are being managed more effectively. Resist the temptation to think of hospitalizations as negative. They're necessary to manage your loved one's disease progression so that he or she can live their remaining days with comfort and as much quality as possible.

Sadness was another emotion I felt whenever Nana went into hospital. Sorrow often washed over me whenever I released her to the care of hospital staff. She was in the best of hands of course and where she needed to be but there was something about leaving her there that always broke my heart. The hospital reminded me of Nana's limited time and I also knew she would rather be at home.

Whether you're actively caregiving at home or caregiving in a more passive fashion while your loved one is in hospital, a wide variety of thoughts and emotions will come to the fore. Expect them and know they'll move on in their own time.

Hospital Admissions as Practice Drills

If your loved one is admitted into hospital due to a significant medical event, a series of ups and downs await you. Death looms large in the background and your fears may stretch like bubblegum, threatening to *pop* into a sticky mess of frayed nerves. If your loved one is eventually discharged, you might choose to consider their hospitalization as a practice drill for the final admission in which he or she won't return home. Some caregivers and their loved ones are given many practice drills while others get no rehearsal at all. There are no fortune-tellers working at the hospital so take each medical episode as they come. Remember, the palliative care team is there to support you in any way they can. Don't keep your concerns to yourself. Communicate openly and honestly. Awards aren't given for soldiering through troubling thoughts and feelings only to collapse in a heap later. Be kind to yourself.

Coughing with alternating chills and fever, my grandmother was hospitalized with pneumonia. No-one thought she'd survive. Sorrow and grief hit me like a ton of bricks. I broke down and tearfully thanked Nana for being such a wonderful grandmother. I felt distraught, thinking this was happening far too fast for me. My emotions were struggling to keep up. Although Nana was elderly and unwell, I simply wasn't ready to lose her. A doctor took me aside to inform me that medication might possibly prolong her life but the decision to treat her was up to me. It was a weighty question. Looking at my grandmother as she lay in bed unable to hear us, I knew she wanted to move on to her next adventure. Unlike other patients, she'd been fortunate to live a long life. But it crushed me to tell the doctor not to give her any medication other than what was necessary for comfort care. I felt I had personally signed Nana's death warrant.

A few days passed and my beloved grandmother was still alive. Listening carefully to Nana's lung sounds, the doctor told me they were distinctly clearer. My grandmother seemed to be coming out of the dark woods and recovering from pneumonia without medical intervention. Neither her doctors nor myself could believe it! She was 95 years old, extremely frail, and wracked with end-stage cancer. Knowing I had a wicked sense of humor, the doctor took me aside and said, "Torie, you couldn't kill her if you wanted to!" We had a good laugh over that. But it had been an awful few days. Believing beyond doubt that Nana was going to die and then having her recover, exposed my aunt (who was there) and myself to extreme emotions. We were exhausted! Later, I decided to consider the pneumonia episode as a 'practice drill' for the final curtain call. It gave me an idea of what to expect should something similar happen again and it gave me the opportunity to consider ways in which I might calm myself in the future.

Hospital Means Respite for You

As a caregiver, hospitalizations can be an opportunity to experience relief from the countless daily tasks you would normally engage in. Take advantage of these moments to rest and regroup. Objectively consider any issues you may have been wrestling with when your loved one had been home. It's easier to brain-storm solutions to problems while he or she is in hospital. Also, if you need to make any purchases for the house, now is a good time to do that.

Whenever Nana was in hospital, I was able to sleep through the night which was unheard of whenever she was home. The extra sleep was absolute paradise! Cooking only for myself, I could eat a hot meal without interruption and pamper myself with long hot showers. At night, I could watch a television program, read a book, or write poetry. It wasn't all fun and games though. I also cleaned the house more thoroughly and tackled my list of household maintenance and repairs.

My grandmother's hospital thoughtfully offered therapeutic massages for the caregivers of their patients. Accept opportunities to unwind if they present themselves to you. I gratefully did. Although I'm not sure how easy it was for the massage therapist to work on my tight muscles. He probably thought he was massaging concrete! Forget using hands and fingers, this fellow needed a jackhammer to relieve my built-up tension!

Exposure to Death

Depending upon the frequency and duration of your loved one's hospitalizations, you may possibly be exposed to the deaths of other patients and witness families grieving in the immediate aftermath. Unlike staff who are trained and experienced in working closely with death and dying, you may find yourself struggling to process and accept the prevalence of it. Exposure to death may depend in part, upon the hospital or facility in which your loved one is a patient. Additionally, your personal, prior experiences with death will also factor into the ways in which it may affect you.

My grandmother had numerous hospitalizations during the last year of her life making exposure to death unavoidable for me. Up to that point, my personal experiences with death had involved family members who tended to die quickly or unexpectedly – out of sight. This made my grandmother's frequent hospitalizations, her slow dying, and exposure to the death of others quite challenging for me. Your situation and background may be entirely different.

However, should you find yourself upset by anything you see or hear while your loved one is hospitalized, speak with a member of the palliative care team.

If Your Loved One Shares a Room

As an in-patient, Nana always shared a room with up to three other women. Over the course of time, these lovely ladies grew well acquainted with one another. Occasionally, one of them would deteriorate and be moved to a private room in order to pass away surrounded by family. My grandmother never asked questions when a roommate disappeared. Death's presence lingered in each room and there wasn't anything anyone could do about it.

Be aware of your loved one's emotions regarding the death of a roommate if he or she shares a room with others. These men and women have serious or terminal illness in common with one another and can bond quite easily by virtue of that. When roommates die, their loss is felt by your loved one and is a poignant reminder of their own mortality.

Give Your Loved One Breaks

Days or weeks as an in-patient can be terribly long for your loved one. Finding ways to break up the long hours of their day is important to their psychological well-being. It's also a way of spending quality time together without the busyness of the multi-tasking that occurs at home. Those of us who are healthy and not enduring terminal illness can only imagine what thoughts and emotions hospitalizations may trigger. Despite the distractions of a bustling medical facility, your loved one may experience a sense of aloneness and a feeling of being unsettled. As caregivers, we are no longer with our loved ones 24/7 while he or she is hospitalized. Our familiar presence, along with the comforts of home are likely missed.

Whenever possible, I took my grandmother beyond the confines of her room. We embarked upon adventurous wheelchair expeditions to explore other floors and lounge areas, admiring gorgeous window views of Botany Bay and Sydney's distant skyscrapers. We watched flocks of ibises fly past; their long, curved beaks looking like elongated noses growing from their small faces. Often, we'd go downstairs to the cafeteria where I'd buy her a slice of madeira cake with lemon icing. On our ventures down long hallways, we'd stop and admire art hanging on the walls; daydreaming about the paintings we'd like to 'walk into.' Nana enjoyed those wheelchair outings. She needed them.

Occasionally, I wheeled my grandmother to the chapel, a serene sanctuary with beautiful stained-glass windows and blue carpet. One morning in the chapel Nana quietly asked, "I wonder if this is what heaven is like?" I paused with a lump in my throat before answering, "Yes, I'm sure it is." Then she softly uttered one word, "Peaceful." I nodded in agreement, not knowing what else to say. Probably because I knew Nana was going to that peaceful place soon and I couldn't imagine us not being together.

Below, are a few suggestions for breaking up your loved one's day while he or she is hospitalized:

- Read a book, magazine, or newspaper together.
- Bring a small radio or iPod and play music as long as it doesn't disturb other patients and their visitors.
- Take wheelchair tours of the hospital – other floors, patient lounge, outdoor garden, chapel, gift shop.
- Work on a small puzzle.
- Watch television together – talk shows, sitcoms, sports, or the news.
- Play board games or cards. But avoid strip poker or forming an illegal gambling ring!
- Eat in the cafeteria. Chat over tea or coffee.
- Encourage other family members and friends to visit. This is a good idea whenever there's a day in which you're unable to visit the hospital.

There is no remedy for love,
But to love more.

Henry David Thoreau

Nursing Home Conversations

Let's revisit this important topic as it will arise repeatedly during your caregiving journey and like a cut gemstone, there are many facets to it. While your loved one is hospitalized, a social worker will likely visit to discuss current and future concerns including the possibility of a nursing home placement as well as your loved one's ability to make their own decisions. These discussions help crystalize current needs and expectations going forward. No-one on the palliative care team wants either of you to fall through the cracks. Engage fully in conversations with social workers. They understand the unique challenges involved in end-of-life care.

The subject of possible nursing home placement for my grandmother was raised during one of her admissions. Nana was unyielding about remaining at home and I was trying hard to keep her there. But unfortunately, over time, my health was being affected and it was obvious that I was nearing the end of my rope as her caregiver. Although she was physically small, lifting Nana for toileting, getting her into and out of bed, or even a chair was becoming difficult. My back was screaming in pain. Nana was so weak that she was a dead weight – no pun intended! Increasingly exhausted from sleep-deprivation and stress, I could barely walk a straight line. Nana deserved a level of care that I could barely provide on my own. The palliative care team knew this and had spoken to Nana and myself many times regarding their concerns. Towards the end, Nana's doctor told me she was no longer worried about my grandmother but she was worried about me.

My aunt and I felt sick to our stomachs but reluctantly made an appointment to speak with the manager of a nursing home located in Nana's community. We had questions to ask and wanted to tour the facility before making a final decision. Nana died on the day of that appointment. She had dodged a bullet, so to speak. I'm grateful for her sake that her long-held wish to avoid a nursing home had come to fruition. But not knowing what lay ahead, I had mentioned it to my grandmother a few days before she passed away. After she died, I agonized over doing so. I wondered whether her final few days were spent worrying about it.

As in the above example, self-doubts and regrets so easily occur in the wake of our caregiving experience. We may long for a second chance to do something differently. Life is full of "If only I had or hadn't _____" (fill in the blank). In the end, acceptance of what was and what is, is necessary for healing. As caregivers, we must find ways to forgive ourselves for simply doing our best under emotional duress. We must find ways to suspend self-judgement and subsequent sentencing. We must make peace with being human.

When Your Loved One Wants to Return Home

During any hospital admission, it's possible your loved one may ask to go home sooner than doctors would advise. Certainly, most of us would prefer to return home quickly no matter what brought us into the hospital to begin with – a broken ankle, a nose job, or gallstones the size of boulders! We long for the familiar, comforting, and ho-hum routine of home. For our loved one whose time on earth is limited, the desire to return home may speak of a deeper need. Listen to his or her concerns as well as listening to what is not being said. Your loved one's soft pleading will fill your heart with compassion at their helplessness. However, it's important for them to remain in hospital until he or she is sufficiently stable for discharge. Let your loved one know that returning home too soon may result in another admission.

Although my grandmother was familiar with the palliative care hospital and had requested to die there (if possible), she often wanted to come back home. The desire to return home became more common with each additional admission and worsened during longer stays. She pleadingly asked doctors, nurses, and myself if she could go home, becoming increasingly emotional. My heart broke to see Nana's tears and imagine how powerless she must have felt. What was it like knowing those around you control almost every aspect of your life? Even though Nana trusted us, respected us, loved us – what must this loss of control, after a lifetime of having it, feel like? Now that my grandmother is gone, I ask myself these questions in retrospect in a desire for greater understanding and clarity of the challenges she faced. If you're reading this book, you have the opportunity to appreciate your loved one's helplessness while he or she still with you.

Our loved ones may also become more aware of their own passing when admitted into hospital and sense this moment may soon be at hand. They need our comforting presence and reassurance that they're not alone. One day, a caregiver will look into your face the way you now look into the face and eyes of your loved one. What words or gestures would comfort you? Consider that, then say those words and make those gestures to the one you hold dear.

When you feel like you CAN'T go any further,
Just know that the strength that carried you this far
Will take you the rest of the way.

Author Unknown

Bring Humor to the Hospital

Carry your sense of humor in your back pocket and reach for it often. Find something to laugh at even if it means looking hard for it. Humor has value and is often underused in serious situations. Laughter is good for us. Our muscles relax, we release happy chemicals, and for at least a moment, our burdens lighten.

On one of the many road trips transporting Nana to the hospital, I was sitting up front next to the ambulance driver while the other paramedic was in the back with my grandmother. After about ten minutes travel I realized I'd left Nana's tiny green suitcase filled with her nightgowns and toiletries back at the house. I knew she wouldn't be happy when she found out and unfortunately, I wouldn't be able to bring her suitcase to the hospital until the following day. After Nana was properly admitted, nurses provided her with pajamas that were far too large. Even a hippopotamus would have had room to grow in them but they were the only size available. Nana was swallowed in layers of fabric! One look from her told me I was sentenced to the dog house for the next decade! When the doctor arrived to examine her, Nana unhappily mentioned not having her own nightgown, toothbrush, and other personal belongings. The doctor shot a glance at me while listening to my grandmother's diatribe. I was guilty as charged but interrupted the conversation pointing out, "Well, it could be worse, I could have brought the suitcase but forgot my grandmother!" That made everyone laugh including Nana and took the edge off the inconvenience she felt.

Discharge Blues

Although your loved one will be eager to return to the comforts of home, their discharge from hospital may mean more work for you and a period of readjustment. You've had a measure of respite and now you'll hit the ground running!

Whenever Nana returned home from hospital, we had to settle into a new routine. She came home stable but weaker. This made sense as her cancer was slowly gaining the upper-hand. There were also greater demands and responsibilities placed upon me. As an in-patient, my grandmother had grown accustomed to the efficiency of the full palliative care team assisting her as necessary around the clock. Back home there was only one person - me. This required more patience from her as I couldn't do multiple tasks simultaneously nor as quickly as the army of people back at the hospital. With each discharge, I was becoming more aware of my own limitations and as Nana's sole caregiver that worried me. Fortunately, after a few days, we both got used to our new routine together. Although my respite was over, I had missed my grandmother's presence around the house and it was good to have her back. Our days together were precious.

Often, Nana was sick in the days immediately following her discharge. This was possibly due to down-sizing from many nurses and instant medications to only having me. But sometimes I also wondered whether she'd been entirely honest with her doctor regarding how well she felt prior to discharge. As an in-patient, Nana would rally herself at the *slightest* possibility of coming home. I'm sure my tiny grandmother would have attempted somersaults or gladly gone scuba diving in Botany Bay in order to prove she was well enough for discharge!

Following your loved one's release from hospital, you too, may notice your loved one growing frailer. It's a sad trend as he or she approaches the end of their life. Unfortunately, this will also translate into more work on your part. Monitor yourself as well as your loved one and keep the palliative care team informed as to how you're both doing.

Practical Tips

1. *Make a list*

Make a list items to bring to the hospital *before* you find yourself in a situation that requires you go there quickly. Hospital admissions, particularly if they're urgent can cause anxiety.

Being ready with a list ahead of time will help you not to forget anything important.

You will need two lists - a list of items your loved one might need and a list of items you may need for yourself should you be at the hospital longer than expected.

List for Your Loved One:

- List of current medications and dosages including any known allergies.
- Your loved one's medical insurance card.
- Medical Power of Attorney/Advanced directives paperwork including a DNR order if you have one.
- Phone numbers of family and friends.
- Hair brush and comb.
- Toothbrush, toothpaste, denture cup.
- Pajamas or nightgown, dressing gown.
- Bed socks and slippers.
- Box of tissues.
- Shaver.
- Reading glasses.
- Hearing-aid & spare batteries.
- Incontinence aids (although the hospital will have them also).
- Hand lotion and lip balm.
- Soap and shampoo.
- Magazines or book.
- Candy, fruit, and other food (if allowed).

List for Yourself:

- Bring a list of important contact information.
- Mobile phone and charger.

- Your own medications if you suspect you may be at the hospital overnight.
- Money for meals, snacks, or coffee at the cafeteria, and a return taxi if you don't have a car.
- Change of underwear and socks (in case you find yourself staying overnight).
- Comfortable clothes you can layer.
- Hair brush or comb.
- Reading glasses.
- Lip balm and small tube of hand lotion. The antibacterial soap at hospitals can really dry your skin.
- Snacks and a bottle of water.
- A small book - perhaps a collection of comforting sayings, poems, or prayers. You may not be able to concentrate on reading but a book in which you can turn to any page and quickly find something calming certainly doesn't hurt.

One important consideration regarding hospital admissions concerns any pets that may need to be cared for while you and your loved one are away. Will the pet end up being left without food and water? Will it need to be taken outside to go potty? Make sure you have someone willing to be available on short notice to look after any pets.

2. *Toiletries*

Be aware that some hospitals prefer patients provide their own toiletries while other hospitals will provide them for you.

3. Leave Valuables at Home

Do not bring valuables to the hospital. This includes credit cards and excessive cash and leave them with your loved one.

4. Contact Community Nursing Services

If your love one uses the services of a community nurse, inform them whenever your loved one is admitted into hospital, otherwise the nurse may arrive at your home ringing the doorbell and wondering where everyone is. Likewise, remember to let them know when your loved one has been discharged so that services can start back up.

5. Contact Medical Alert Device Company

If your loved one wears a Medical Alert device, contact the company to let them know your loved one will be in hospital and no longer using it while admitted. Otherwise, the company may run a scheduled test of its services while your loved one (and you) are away. This might trigger the company to believe something is wrong when no-one answers and send an ambulance to an empty home! Be sure to let the company know when your loved one has returned.

6. Meal-time Discharges

Whenever your loved one is discharged near meal-time consider taking him or her to the hospital's cafeteria to eat rather than going straight home. Otherwise, you'll need to prepare a meal soon after arriving back at the house. Waiting at the hospital for doctors to sign discharge papers can be tiring and if you're like me, you may not feel like cooking or making sandwiches as soon as you walk in the door of your home. Save yourself a little trouble by eating at the cafeteria. Your loved one will enjoy eating in a setting that doesn't resemble their hospital room and you can then return home with nothing to immediately do other than settle your loved one into bed or a chair and then unpack.

7. Prepare Home ahead of Time

Remember to have your loved one's bed sheets and blankets pulled back from their bed should he or she wish to lie down immediately upon arrival home. Sometimes, the taxi or car ride from the hospital can be trying for your loved one and they arrive home feeling a little sick. There may also be one or two new items you might need to purchase as a direct result of your loved one's latest hospitalization including new medications or the same medications with different dosages.

<u>Conversation Starters</u>

It's not easy to be unwell and away from the familiarity of home. Dare to look into your loved one's eyes and see yourself. Love them, listen to them, and comfort them with your caring presence.

What Your Loved One Wants You, Their Caregiver, to Know While He or She is in Hospital:

~ Most of the time, I'm comfortable being here in hospital but sometimes I'm not. The longer I stay and the more often I'm admitted, the more I just want to go back home. Sometimes I'm home only a week or two and then I'm back in hospital again. This upsets me. I want to be surrounded by the familiarity of home. I miss my friends and neighbors. I miss the views from my own windows even though the views from the hospital are lovely.

~ I like the other women/men I share a room with. We can all relate to one another. Their friendship and common circumstances help me cope. But sometimes one of them is wheeled away on their bed and never comes back. I'm always reminded of what my future will be. Waiting for my turn to die causes me to feel anxious at times.

~ I love all the ice-cream I'm given in the hospital but most of all I want to eat the food or candy I'm used to at home. I like it when you bring me a few snacks such as my favorite candy, fruit, or biscuits.

~ I don't like it when you have to leave me to go back home for the night. I wish you could stay longer. I wish you didn't have to go at all. I feel sad when you leave and a little frightened. You're my caregiver, you look after me, and I want you to stay.
~ Sometimes when we're in the gift shop I want you to purchase an item or two on my behalf. It may be an object that I don't need but it gives me a taste of something I've been missing – choice and control. I like buying something with my own money. For a moment, I can pretend that I'm who I used to be.

~ Sometimes, I don't like to bother the nurses because they're busy. I keep my needs to myself rather than tell them that I feel sick, in discomfort, or need to use the toilet. I wait until I can't wait anymore.

~ It's wonderful when the therapy dogs come to visit. I forget about being sick. Patting them calms me and I enjoy listening to their handlers tell me stories.

~ I don't like the taste of the liquid medicine nurses leave in a cup for me to drink. Sometimes I take it into the bathroom and empty it down the sink but don't tell them I do that!

~ I want you to know that I'm grateful each day you come to visit me. Having you sit beside me means a lot. Your presence is comforting and helps to pass the hours with less anxiety.

~ I like it when you walk with me or wheel me down the hall. It's fun to explore other areas of the hospital such as the cafeteria, outdoor garden, or patient lounge. I especially appreciate the peace and tranquility of the chapel. I'm reminded that a Higher Power is with me and I'm not alone.

~ I tell you and the palliative care team that I'm not afraid to die but sometimes I do feel a little scared. Keep reminding me of how wonderful it will be when I'm no longer sick and I can join my loved ones who have gone on before me. Those thoughts comfort me. Also tell me that you'll be alright without me. I worry about you.

Chapter 7

The Final Moment Has Come

> *The heart is right to cry*
> *Even when the smallest drop of light,*
> *Of love,*
> *Is taken away.*
>
> Hafiz

Even as a youngster, I knew I wanted to be by my grandmother's side at the end of her life. Accompanying her to the pearly gates and placing her in God's care was something I always wanted to do. It's as though I needed to make sure she arrived there alright. Over the years, I often wondered if everything would work out the way I hoped it would. What if I lived on the other side of the planet? What if I couldn't get there fast enough? What if I were having an emergency appendectomy at the time? These were things I worried about. In the end, I was by her side, able to be her end-of-life companion and walk her Home.

When the end finally arrives for your dear one, be aware that circumstances may not play themselves out the way you thought they would. Most things in life rarely do. Be open to whatever comes and the way in which it unfolds. When death occurs, you'll already be emotionally and physically drained by virtue of caregiving and may find it hard to wrap your mind around the fact that your loved one has finally passed after all you went through together. It's a strange human quirk that even though we know death is coming and may have watched it happen, the event itself can seem surreal. You've sacrificed many of your own needs for those of your loved one and his or her sudden departure may be hard to fully process. Alternating between heart-break and stunned numbness is common. No matter what occurs or how it happens, losing the person you've been caring for will leave you with a sense of emptiness and profound loss. The challenge moving forward will involve filling this inner void with love, compassion, and the best of memories.

The Call

Unless you're at the hospital during the time your loved one begins actively dying, you'll receive a phone call alerting you that he or she has "taken a turn for the worse." Although such news is not unexpected, the announcement may shake you to the core.

The call can come at any time. In the middle of the night, the ringing telephone will cause your brain to think 'hospital' and you'll suspect the nature of the call before you pick up the phone. But if contact comes during the day, you may answer and expect to hear the voice of a friend or family member. If the daytime call *is* from the hospital you might be thinking it's to alert you that your loved one has taken another fall or to ask whether you've had a chance to read the paperwork you were given regarding nursing homes. We usually don't think, 'This is it,' when the telephone rings during the day. Often, we think our loved one's inevitable passing is an event that's always one or two small steps in front of us – just out of reach. "Not today. Please not today. I'm not ready. Tomorrow might be better." But we can't prevent or postpone the inevitable. Nature has been following its own course for eons. Dying has been inseparable from living, since living first began.

Contemplate the possible scenarios in which a telephone call from the hospital might come so that you're not entirely taken by surprise. After you hang up you may be shaking like a leaf. Who else will you need to call? Another family member or friend? Will you need a taxi to take you to the hospital or do you have a car? If you have a car, will you be able to drive safely or will you need someone else to drive? What items will you need to grab quickly to bring with you? Is there a pet who will need looking after? These are a few questions to ponder before the call from the hospital actually comes.

In my case, it was early evening when a hospital nurse called and gently broke the news that Nana had "taken a turn for the worse." Apparently, my grandmother had a seizure following dinner and was unresponsive. Staff had taken her to a private room. My heart began pounding and my hands shook. One part of my brain knew exactly what this meant but the other part needed a little more time. I stalled, asking, "Is this something that could end my grandmother's life?" I already knew the answer. "So, I should take a taxi, pick up my aunt, and come to the hospital right now?" Again, I already knew the answer. No more stalling, no more hoping the phone call was a mistake. This was it. The journey that had been Nana's long and amazing life was now coming to an end. I felt my body turn to jelly. My fingers trembled as I pushed the buttons on the telephone to make a quick call to my mother in the United States and to my aunt who lived nearby.

Sitting in the back seat of the taxi with my aunt, my mind was in a fog. I couldn't concentrate on the scenery we were passing. Emotionally, I didn't feel ready for this. Perhaps no-one ever feels truly prepared.

Walking down the long hospital hallway I could *hear* my grandmother before we entered her room. Her respiratory system was making a sound I had previously heard other dying patients make as their bodies fought to continue living. Hearing Nana breathe like that crushed me. She was really dying this time. No more practice drills, the ties that bound her to this earthly residence were unravelling. I was deeply saddened and afraid, wondering what her death was going to be like and whether I could handle it.

I'm a flower, Poa,
A flower opening and reaching
For the sun.

You are the sun, Grandma,
You are the sun in my life.

Kitty   Tsui

Comfort Care not Life-Extending Care

Patients who've experienced an acute medical event such as a stroke or who've been injured in a car accident for example, are usually hooked up to a tangle of tubes and beeping monitors. But this jungle of noisy equipment usually isn't attached to terminally ill patients within palliative care facilities. You may be surprised by the absence of visible equipment. As your loved one dies, he or she is given comfort care as opposed to traditional life-extending or life-saving care. Alleviating pain, nausea, and anxiety as well as other symptoms is the primary focus of medical staff charged with monitoring your loved one as they die.

Nurses will also regularly wash your loved one as they lay in bed and change their undergarments, pajamas, or nightgowns if necessary. Your loved one will remain clean throughout the dying process. Should you have any concerns or questions regarding their comfort care speak with doctors and nurses. They'll gladly explain everything they're doing or not doing. Seek to understand rather than risk misunderstanding. The palliative care team assisted you and your loved one in the past and they won't abandon you now. Communicate with them.

Looking After Yourself

Waiting bedside and watching your loved one for hours or days on end is emotionally and physically draining. It's important to find ways to care for yourself during this difficult time. Stay hydrated by drinking plenty of water especially if you're drowning in tears. Remember to stand and stretch your legs periodically just as you would on a long flight overseas. While you may not always feel hungry, you do need to eat something throughout the day even if it's simply a snack. Use the hospital chapel if you need a few moments in a quiet and peaceful setting. You can also ask to speak with a chaplain or pastoral care worker. Pastoral care staff are likely to visit with you and your family regardless, to determine whether there is anything you need. If you're a praying person – include yourself in those prayers. Your loved one still needs your strength. You are still his or her caregiver.

What if My Loved One Passes When I Leave Their Room?

Doctors and nurses prepared me for the possibility that my grandmother might pass away whenever I left her room. I was bedside 98% of the time but sometimes I left briefly to stretch my legs or walk to the patient lounge for a cup of tea or coffee. Occasionally, I went downstairs to the cafeteria to grab a bite to eat, often bringing food back to Nana's room. Never gone long, I was aware that I might miss something important each time I stepped beyond her door.

For some families and individuals, their loved one does pass away when they leave the room. You might sit by your loved one's bedside for hours on end and the instant you walk outside he or she decides to move on to their next adventure. Should this happen, please know that your caregiving journey with your loved one isn't diminished in any way by your absence at the very end. Perhaps your loved one wanted to spare you in some way. Make peace with any thoughts and feelings that accompany this occurrence including any sadness, disappointment, and anger. Don't allow the ending to ruin the entire story. It's no-one's fault – not yours and not your loved ones. Should you feel even a smidgeon of guilt for having left the room, forgive yourself and move forward. None of us have any control over death's timetable. We *plan* to be with our loved one at the very end only to have death remind us that our plans are made of paper mâché and never etched in marble. No matter how well-meaning our intentions, circumstances may play out differently. Pastoral care and bereavement counsellors can help you process your feelings if you need assistance.

Let me not squander
The hours of my pain.

Rainer Maria Rilke

Communicate Your Love

Be mindfully present with your loved one while they are dying. Even if his or her eyes are closed and they appear unresponsive, your loved one can still *hear* the sound of your voice. Let him or her know you love them and that it's alright for them to go whenever they're ready. Let him or her know that you'll be alright and will see them again. Give your loved one as much emotional and spiritual support as you can. Ultimately, this moment of transitioning is about them. Indeed, you will be alright although you may not feel that way now. Remember, there are those who will love and support you in the difficult days, weeks, and months ahead. For now, assist your loved one in having as peaceful and comfortable a passing as possible. Surround him or her with love. Hold their tender hand, stroke their soft hair, sing them a song, or massage their skin with lotion. Some families play soothing music for their loved one while they're dying. As his or her caregiver, you know your loved one well, do and say what you think would comfort them.

Acts of Kindness

It was early Saturday evening when the hospital called me regarding my grandmother. On the following Monday morning, weekday staff and volunteers arrived, hearing the news that Nana was truly passing away this time. My aunt and I were in her room, exhausted having been at the hospital that entire time. Out of the corner of our weary eyes we noticed movement and heard a soft knock on the doorframe. Walking over, I was deeply touched to find a line of volunteers wearing pale blue shirts respectfully enquiring whether they might take a moment to say good-bye to my grandmother. Over the course of Nana's numerous hospitalizations, they knew her well. These dedicated individuals had shared stories with her, laughed together, and given Nana at least a million arm and leg massages which she loved. Nana had a genuine soft-spot for these volunteers and apparently the feeling was mutual.

Standing back against the wall. My aunt and I looked on as volunteers took turns saying goodbye to my grandmother. They whispered in her ear, held her hand, and softly touched her face. One quietly recited the rosary. How wonderful for my grandmother to receive such gifts of the heart! My aunt and I were consoled by these acts of kindness. A lovely Scottish volunteer asked if she could give Nana one last leg massage. She lifted the blue blankets from the foot of the bed and gently rubbed my grandmother's pencil-thin legs. Massages were one of Nana's favorite things, aside from eating candy, and I know this tender human touch was comforting for her. I was aware that choosing to massage Nana's legs one final time must not have been easy for this volunteer. She didn't have to do it. Hers was an act of compassion. The memories of those kind volunteers as well as other members of the palliative care team who quietly came to say goodbye throughout the day will always remain in my heart.

You too, will witness and experience acts of kindness from staff and volunteers. Remember these gentle moments. These memories will comfort you for many years to come.

At this time of my parting,
Wish me good luck, my friends!
The sky is flushed with the dawn
And my path lies beautiful.

Rabindranath Tagore

Final Words

You may or may not hear your loved one utter final words of significance. Passing away isn't like the movies we watch on television in which the person dying speaks softly, saying something important such as who the real killer is, where the gold is hidden, or don't let little Johnny forget me. As death approaches, many patients are simply too weak to speak while others may indeed try to communicate with you. It's also possible that your loved one may say things that don't make sense to you. Confusion can occur as his or her dying brain experiences chemical changes. Don't count upon hearing meaningful words but if you're blessed to hear them spoken, cherish them.

My grandmother was too feeble to speak. She barely moved a muscle. I felt such sadness knowing I'd never hear her soft voice again. But on the final day of her life, Nana began making sounds as though trying to speak. I had the impression she didn't want my aunt or I to go home as we had always done when visiting her during previous admissions. Trying to engage her with what I thought was her concern I asked, "Nana, do you want us to stay?" Of course, we were staying regardless. Right away she nodded. Then very softly said, "Mm . . . stay." I asked her again and again she answered the same way but a little louder. I was excited knowing she seemed to be having a lucid moment and was able to quietly speak. I told her several times that we'd stay with her and would not go home. She seemed relieved. Then with eyes full of tears, I said, "I love you Nana." She immediately replied, "I love you too." Those were her final words and a beautiful parting gift to me. A moment later, my aunt who had briefly stepped outside of Nana's room came back in. I told her Nana had spoken. Surprised, my aunt hurried over to the bed and began talking to her mother but sadly Nana never spoke again. I wish there'd been a way to squeeze a few more words out of my grandmother for my aunt's sake. But Nana was too weak and too tired to say more.

Even as I stood there, the tears streaming
Down my face, I felt a kind of joy for him,
A strange gaiety for him almost,
That he would soon be released,
And I had a sense that he stood now
On the threshold of some great adventure ...
So it was in a strange way not only a time
Of terrible sorrow, but a moment of light,
As I stood there telling him goodbye.

Martha Whitmore Hickman

Use Humor to Break the Tension

Despite death's presence, find something light and humorous to temporarily lift the emotional weight of the situation. Humor can break the tension, giving your grieving heart much-needed breathing-space. The heaviness of watching a loved one die is enormous. Minute by minute, hour after hour, the pressure builds. While your wet, weary eyes focus upon your loved one's face and the slow-moving clock on the wall, your heart braces for emotional impact. Finding something to smile about or laugh at in a situation such as this can be a huge stress reliever. Humor isn't disrespectful to the dying. Allowing your loved one to hear laughter and sense that you're going to be fine, lets them leave with less worry. Your loved one wants to know that you'll make it through this difficult time and go on to live a good life until you both meet again.

In earlier chapters, I've mentioned my grandmother's incurable sweet tooth. Family and friends teased her mercilessly for it. While unwell and baulking at most foods, Nana usually continued eating candy, chocolate, and cake with sugary icing. During each hospital admission, my aunt and I maintained a steady supply of sweets for her in the drawer beside her bed. When I knew Nana was dying, I felt she needed some sugar 'for the road' and I placed a pink marshmallow on the pillow near her head. The little marshmallow brought a touch of levity. I'm not sure whether Nana was aware of the marshmallow's presence. Perhaps the sweet scent was familiar and comforting or perhaps she wanted to choke me because she was too weak to reach up and grab it! Either way, I knew Nana would have enjoyed the humor behind my silly gesture.

On Nana's final evening, my aunt and I found ourselves quite hungry. The cafeteria was closed but the kitchen staff who cook for patients kindly made a meal for us. We were touched by their thoughtfulness and our growling stomachs were quite appreciative. My aunt and I sat on either side of two large trays of food and drinks while a nurse put the television on for us. Funny enough, Nana's favorite rugby team, the St. George

Dragons were playing a match. We turned the television monitor to face Nana so that she could watch it as well. Although Nana's lovely pale blue eyes were open, my aunt and I were unsure of the clarity of her vision or the state of her mental consciousness but watching rugby was something commonplace for her. It was something she would have done had she been home that night. We hoped she had some awareness and that the sounds of the rugby match were familiar and consoling.

Utterly famished, my aunt and I dug into our delicious food with full abandon! It was so good to eat a proper meal and wonderful having the television on. We'd been isolated from the rest of the world for the past few days and for a moment, we were mentally transported somewhere else, somewhere that felt more home-like. Several minutes or more passed by and suddenly, I remembered Nana! Quickly looking at her, I found to my great relief that she was still breathing! I recall shaking my head while giggling and saying to my aunt, "Nana could have been dead for the past 20 minutes for all we knew! Here we are filling our faces and watching TV!" We had a good laugh at our tired selves. Emotionally, my aunt and I needed that break from relentless, sorrowful reality. It was Monday evening and we'd already been at the hospital around-the-clock since Saturday. We looked and felt a wreck! Luckily nothing happened to my grandmother while our attention was diverted elsewhere but I do believe that had she passed, Nana would have known my aunt and I were enjoying ourselves. She would have looked down upon us, rolled her eyes, and laughed! Then she would have wondered whether the Dragons were winning the rugby game!

Laughter is the sun that drives
Winter from the human face.

Victor Hugo

The Dying Process – What to Expect

Our brains have strong survival instincts and usually attempt to orchestrate last-ditch efforts on our behalf. It doesn't matter to our brain that the odds of survival are insurmountable. It doesn't matter that cancer or some other disease has eaten us alive or that our organs are failing. Looking at it objectively, our bodies are quite remarkable. But as living bags of water we aren't designed or built to last forever.

Your loved one's body will undergo many changes throughout the dying process. Here are just a few:

- o Changes in your loved one's breathing will be the most notable difference. Breaths may be shallow and rapid or may have long intervals in between.
- o Fluid accumulating in the back of the throat often results in a gargling, gurgling sound. In the old days, this noise was ominously referred to as the 'death rattle.' The fluid accumulation is usually not uncomfortable for your loved one.
- o Your loved one will have lost their appetite and will no longer eat or drink.
- o As you hold your loved one's hand, you'll notice his or her fingertips growing cool to the touch. With time, this coolness will spread throughout their entire hand. This is also true of their feet. Your loved one's circulation is slowing down.
- o Your loved one will sleep for increasing periods of time.
- o Sometimes, a loved one may appear agitated or grow restless as his or her brain loses oxygen. Medication can be given to relax him or her should this occur.

It's unpleasant to think about these bodily changes especially while your loved one is still alive. But as his or her caregiver, it's important to know what you may see or hear as you sit beside your loved one while they are passing. Now is not the time to be caught unawares. You've experienced enough stress as it is. Your loved one's body is battle-weary and now it's time for him or her to rest. The palliative care team will share information with you as death approaches. Of course, not everyone wants to understand the physiological processes involved in dying. Let the team know how you feel. Personally, I found it helpful to understand what I was seeing and hearing. You may feel otherwise. The main thing is to give your special someone plenty of love in the time remaining.

Doctors and nurses will do their utmost to assist your loved one in having a gentle passing. However, let go of expectations and assumptions of what dying should look and sound like especially if you're new to it. Instead, take each moment with your loved one as it presents itself. Trust the palliative care team to step in when they need to. But if you notice any discomfort, anxiety, agitation, or confusion on the part of your loved one alert staff immediately. They'll quickly reduce any unpleasant symptoms. Also keep in mind that what's comfortable for your loved one at one moment, may not be comfortable in an hour's time. His or her body is changing and no longer stabilizing. Ring the bedside buzzer attached to your loved one's bed and keep nurses informed when you notice anything new or troublesome. They'll do what's in their power to maintain your loved one's comfort but each case is different and every 'body' reacts differently as it passes from this earth.

Just when the caterpillar
Thought the world was over,
It became a butterfly.

Author Unknown

My Grandmother's Passing

Everything seemed surreal; a strange and sad dream that I couldn't wake up from. Nothing was familiar. Standing upon new territory, I was enclosed by a landscape that I had dreaded my entire life. Although trying to be brave, my fear felt large as I tried stuffing as much of it as I could into some distant part of my brain. I couldn't risk falling apart. I needed to be 'present' for my grandmother's sake, after all, we had a journey to complete together. I also needed to be strong for my aunt, widowed only a year, and now watching her mother die.

My grandmother's body went through many changes as it slowly released its hold on life. Her consciousness however, her thoughts and feelings during this time were more of a mystery due to her inability to communicate. Repeatedly, I reminded her of the enormous love that surrounded her.

A small amount of bubbly white froth began collecting upon Nana's lips a few hours after my aunt and I arrived at the hospital. It was fluid from her lungs and normal in the dying process. Using large cotton-swabs, a nurse soaked up the fluids inside her mouth but shortly after walking away, the frothing started again. This time it was worse. I grabbed a few extra swabs the nurse had left behind and began soaking up the fluids myself hoping the flow would stop. It didn't. Plan B involved giving Nana medication to dry the secretions. Fortunately, the medication worked quickly and she seemed comfortable.

Over time, my grandmother's fingertips became cool to the touch, losing their natural warmth. Noticing these physical changes filled me with deep sadness. Her body was dying and ready-or-not I was a spectator, helpless to do anything about it other than give her my love. Many prayers came to my lips, not only for Nana but for family who weren't able to be there by her side but who loved her dearly. That first night, I slept on my grandmother's bed curled up beside her. Precious moments passed, listening to her breathe and feeling the movements of her chest until I dozed off from fatigue.

As she sought precious air, my grandmother made gurgling sounds at times. These became more frequent and louder as she approached what would be her final evening. Believing Nana wasn't in any distress, the sounds didn't bother me until I noticed her trying to sit up and cough, as though to clear her throat. Unfortunately, she was too weak to do either. Thinking Nana might be feeling uncomfortable, I called a nurse who suggested suctioning in order to remove the excessive secretions. Shortly thereafter, two nurses with suctioning equipment asked my aunt and I to wait outside the room. When we re-entered, there was a significant decrease in gargling sounds. Nana no longer tried to cough or sit up. Relieved for her sake, I hoped she would now have another few hours of easier breathing. But she passed away shortly thereafter. Later, I found myself questioning whether the suctioning had inadvertently hastened her death. Should I have mentioned to nurses that Nana seemed to be trying to sit up and cough? If I hadn't told them, would she have lived an hour longer? A few hours longer? Was suctioning uncomfortable for her? I struggled with these questions. But of course, alerting nurses to Nana's possible discomfort was the right thing to do. I mention this to illustrate the second-guesses and worries we may later experience. Being by our loved one's side as they die isn't easy and sometimes, we may query certain aspects of it. This is normal when in the midst of emotionally charged circumstances. Make peace with uncertainty. Neither birth nor death is an exact science and we are all striving to do our best for those entering or leaving this world.

Soon after suctioning but prior to Nana's passing, my aunt and I laid down upon reclining chairs near her bed. We were exhausted. Suddenly, I realized Nana's breathing had become very quiet. I jumped up and dashed to the side of her bed sensing the end was near. My aunt joined me. My grandmother's lips began gently moving up and down the way a fish's mouth moves when it's taken out of water. Her old, cancer-riddled body was trying desperately to take in oxygen. Then her lips stopped moving. For a moment, nothing happened. Nana was quiet. Not knowing if she were still alive, I gently pulled back the bedsheets from her chest and watched for movement. Suddenly, her chest rose high as though she had taken in a deep breath. Then it fell and never rose again. Taking her pulse, I felt nothing other than the racing of my own heart. I looked at my aunt and shook my head telling her Nana was gone and pushed the bedside buzzer for the nurse.

Feeling shaky, I was impatient for the nurse to arrive. Something momentous had just happened and it seemed too large for my aunt and I to endure alone. We needed someone else in the room with us; a professional who could take over. My beloved grandmother had just died and I didn't know what to do about it. I wanted someone to tell me that everything would be alright; that my aunt and I would be alright. When the nurse quietly entered the room, I sensed she already knew what had taken place. I tried to hold my emotions together as I faltered with trembling voice, "I think my grandmother passed away." The nurse walked to the side of the bed, felt for a carotid pulse and then turned to us and nodded. It was 12:25 am – twenty-five minutes into the first day of Spring. A watchful moon hung in the cool night sky outside the window. Below us, moored yachts gently bobbed upon glassy Kogarah Bay and sleepy street lights shimmered. On the inner side of the large pane of glass, my aunt and I were heavy hearted yet relieved for Nana's sake that her journey was over. We lingered with my grandmother, embraced by the night yet aware that dawn would herald a new day; a day missing the one we loved.

Many thoughts and feelings ran through my heart and mind all at once when Nana passed away. I felt partially stunned by the emotional collision. It was hard to fully grasp all that had taken place. Nana's frail body had fought like a gladiator to the very end. She deserved rest now and was finally in her forever Home. My childhood desire to be by my grandmother's side at the end of her life had come true. Now Nana was with the many loved ones that she had missed over the long years of her life – her parents, grandparents, brothers, husband, infant son, and numerous friends. She no longer needed to look at their framed photographs sitting upon the shelves of her little house. She was with them.

Standing alongside my grandmother's hospital bed, it was hard to believe my caregiving journey by her side was now over. Next to me, my aunt stood quietly. She had lost her husband (my Uncle Terry) to colon cancer almost exactly one year earlier at this same hospital and was now saying good-bye to her mother. My heart went out to her for these two significant losses. I also thought of my own mother, Nana's first-born daughter who was back in the U.S. and had been unable to come to Australia. Not being here broke her heart and I knew she was anxiously awaiting news. Her life and my aunt's life would change forever with the loss of someone so dear to them. I thought of my sisters also awaiting news of Nana's passing and although they were expecting this, it would be hard for them to hear she was finally gone. My young nieces were losing their great-grandmother and I wished they'd been able to spend more time with her. There were stories that only Nana could share and knowledge that only she could impart.

> *There is a sacredness in tears.*
> *They are not the mark of weakness,*
> *but of power.*
> *They speak more eloquently*
> *Than ten thousand tongues.*
> *They are the messengers*
> *Of overwhelming grief*
> *… and of unspeakable love.*
>
> Washington Irving

The Immediate Aftermath of Your Loved One's Passing

Nurses will wash your loved one's body at their bedside once he or she has died. You may be asked if you'd like to participate in this gentle cleansing. If you feel up to it, by all means do so. If you don't, that's quite acceptable too. You may also be asked about clean clothes for your loved one or nurses may simply change his or her hospital gown. Each facility is different.

Many hospitals place a rolled washcloth beneath their patient's chin in the moments following their passing. This prevents the relaxed muscles of their mouth from opening. Nurses may also place your loved one's hands together upon their chest. A bible may be opened to Psalm 23, a vase of flowers or a candle placed inside the room. Each hospital has their own way of honoring and respecting your loved one. If you have a specific religious or cultural request, speak with the palliative care team ahead of time. They will endeavor to accommodate your families' traditions. For many, the death of a loved one is a sacred time of reflection and transition.

Taking that last look at your loved one as you leave his or her hospital room for the final time may be one of the most difficult things you do. You may want to linger forever at that doorway. Don't be surprised if a brief fear washes over you, wondering whether you'll forget the details of that beautiful face as soon as you walk past the doorframe. This thought may prompt you to take one more glance, then another, and another. But at some point, you must leave, returning to a house that will feel far too empty and silent.

You had always brought your loved one home following previous hospitalizations. This time, you'll leave hospital without him or her. You'll leave the body you cared for behind – the body you medicated, fed, washed, dressed, and kissed goodnight. Walking away from your loved one's bedside and beyond the front doors of the hospital is a heart-wrenching trail of tears. Simply putting one foot in front of the other is all you might manage.

You will also need to inform family and friends of your loved one's passing if they weren't with you at the time. If your loved one dies in the middle of the night as my grandmother did, you'll be faced with the decision to either wake relatives with the news or call them early in the morning after sunrise.

> *A woman's strength*
> *Isn't just about how much*
> *She can handle before she breaks.*
> *It's also about how much*
> *She must handle after she's broken.*
>
> Author Unknown

Back Home from Hospital

When you arrive home, I recommend making yourself a cup of tea or coffee as soon as you can. Simply sit and take your time drinking it. Perhaps a hot shower and change of clothes will also help you feel better. Yes, there are telephone calls to make but at this juncture, simply rest. Let your tired body and sorrowful heart have that much needed moment of stillness. The hot tea or coffee will give you a modicum of rejuvenation. Your exhausted brain is trying to grasp the momentous event that just occurred and all the weeks, months or years of caregiving that preceded it. All will get done in due time. But for now, take baby steps. Be your own caregiver. Your loved one would want you to do that.

> *Death is not extinguishing the light*
> *It is putting out the lamp*
> *Because the dawn has come.*
>
> Rabindranath Tagore

Bereavement Services

Please consider taking advantage of any bereavement services offered to you. It's tremendously helpful to have a compassionate and understanding professional assist you in honoring your experiences as a grieving caregiver. Bereavement counsellors can guide you as you begin a new chapter of your life. Many hospitals, community centers, and churches offer this assistance. A few weeks after Nana passed away, I sought the bereavement services offered by the hospital where she died. The support I received and insight into the grieving process relational to being a caregiver assisted me greatly in moving forward.

Conversation Starters

From Caregiver to Caregiver, What I'd Like You to Know:

~ Receiving a telephone call from the hospital informing you that your loved one has 'taken a turn for the worse' will jolt your nerves. But you'll survive this upsetting call and make your way safely to the hospital. You're stronger than you know.

~ Observing your loved one's feeble body try so hard to continue living isn't easy to watch. It's difficult to observe the signs of imminent passing but you can do this. Remember, gentle time will heal your pain.

~ Your dear loved one can still hear the sound of your voice. Let him or her know you love them even if your voice trembles and tears wet your face.

~ Being present as your loved one takes his or her final breath is heart-breaking. You might collapse in a heap when it's over but you will find a way to get back on your feet and stand. Don't forget that.

~ If you happen to have left your loved one's room when he or she passes away, you may find yourself feeling disappointed, angry, and sad. Be with your feelings. With time, you'll come to accept this common occurrence. Not being present at the moment of death doesn't diminish your caregiving journey and all that you did for your loved one.

~ Walking away with your loved one's belongings in a large plastic bag while the hospital retains your loved one will seem an unfair exchange. There are so many layers of sadness. Again, you're strong and can do this.

Her absence is like the sky,
Spread over everything.

C.S. Lewis

Psalm 23

The Lord is my shepherd; I shall not want.
He maketh me to lie down in green pastures:
he leadeth me beside the still waters.
He restoreth my soul:
he leadeth me in the paths
of righteousness for his name's sake.
Yea, though I walk
through the shadow of the valley of death,
I will fear no evil: for thou art with me;
thy rod and thy staff they comfort me.
Thou prepareth a table before me
in the presence of mine enemies:
thou anointest my head with oil;
my cup runneth over.
Surely goodness and mercy shall
follow me all the days of my life:
and I will dwell
in the house of the Lord forever.

He Is Not Dead

*I cannot say, and I will not say
That he is dead. He is just away.
With a cheery smile, and a wave of the hand,
He has wandered into an unknown land
And left us dreaming how very fair
It needs must be, since he lingers there.
And you—oh you, who the wildest yearn
For an old-time step, and the glad return,
Think of him faring on, as dear
In the love of There as the love of Here.
Think of him still as the same. I say,
He is not dead—he is just away."*

James Whitcomb Riley

Chapter 8

Life after Caregiving: Traveling Ahead Without Your Loved One

*There will come a time
When your loved one will be gone,
And you will find comfort in the fact
That you were their caregiver.*

Karen Coetzer

Morning has broken upon the horizon of a new day; a new life. Although your eyes may open and fill with tears, your loved one has awoken pain-free – no longer enclosed within a chrysalis of disease and dependence. Like an emerging butterfly, they begin anew; unencumbered and free. You walked him or her Home and they are safe.

After days, weeks, months, or years of experiencing anticipatory grief as a caregiver, you are now bathed in the sorrow of the actual event. You have completed one journey only to begin another. Grief is not only an excursion into the depths of loss, it's also a healing journey. Grief calls us to care for our wounds and give rest to our weariness. It asks us to linger a little longer upon the quiet mountain top and simply BE.

The Early Days and Weeks

Your former purpose, your caregiver role vanished with one gently expelled breath and initially, it may be hard to fully grasp this sweeping change and finality. Yet ready or not, you now begin a new chapter of your life's story, one that does not include your loved one. The first words and paragraphs you tearfully write will speak of loss, sorrow, and emptiness. Yet slowly, with each word you inscribe, with each page you live, there will arise a tale of inner healing and recovery as you move forward beyond your caregiving role.

The days and weeks immediately following your loved one's passing can be a whirlwind of activity and emotions that carry you along for the ride. It can be difficult to find a few minutes to yourself to either rest, regroup, or have a good uninterrupted cry. At the same time, it feels comforting to have so many people reach out in acknowledgment, support, and shared sorrow.

Although there is much to be done, certain duties can be divided among family members. The first order of business is communicating the death of your loved one to those awaiting that sad news. Fortunately, telephone calls, emails, letter writing, and later, sending thank you cards, are tasks easily shared. Spreading the work load, so to speak, makes a huge difference when you're absolutely worn out. Make an attempt to rest, even if it's only for a short period of time. Taking care of yourself is important. Your loved one would want you to do that. He or she is not far away enjoying a heavenly Bahamian vacation, having forgotten all about you. Not at all, honor your loved one by looking after your needs.

Be mindful that friends and relatives who were absent from their loved one's side when they passed away, often wish to know details such as whether he or she suffered at the end. Prepare to share this information over and over, even though the telling of it translates into reliving it. Family and friends need to know what happened in order to make peace with their own loss. They appreciate you sharing this difficult experience with them. Repeatedly narrating your loved one's final moments may also help you process what has occurred especially if you're having trouble wrapping your mind around it.

Another upsetting task involves the clothing your loved one last wore such as pajamas, nightgown, socks, or dressing gown. Will you keep any of them? My aunt and I washed the clothes my grandmother wore in hospital and hung them on the clothesline to dry in the sun. The only things that didn't dry were our tears.

Flowers and sympathy cards will arrive for you daily as word spreads that your loved one has died. Savor the sweet fragrance of the colored blossoms and the comfort they bring. You'll find yourself hoping your loved one is aware of these many beautiful tributes to his or her life. With time, these flowers will begin to wilt until only a few good stems remain; reminding you of how many days it's been since your loved one took his or her final breath. The blossoming and withering of these delicate floras become a symbol of life's never-ending circle. Eventually, with no more flowers to care for or cards arriving, life gently seems to whisper, "It's time to begin anew."

A sadder and wiser man,
He rose the morrow morn.

Samuel Taylor Coleridge

The Business Side of Death

Funeral arrangements are made soon after your loved one passes. You may already have a particular funeral company in mind or previously purchased a pre-paid plan for your loved one. If you're new to this side of death, funeral directors will gently guide you through this process and answer any questions you may have. Depending upon your loved one's final wishes, the next step involves contacting a cemetery or crematorium to arrange for burial or cremation.

Did your loved one want a funeral service? Some individuals decide against a formal service preferring instead that family and friends come together informally and share stories. It's important to know ahead of time what your loved one's final wishes were.

My grandmother didn't want a funeral. She once told me, "No-one would come." I cried remembering her words as I came to discover how much the little community in which she had lived felt the loss of her gentle soul. Nana didn't seem to realize how many lives she had touched. Betty, one of my grandmother's friends, opened her small home to several of Nana's neighbors and mates. We had a wonderful yet sad time remembering all the many things we loved about my grandmother. A long table was laden with Nana's favorite foods and candy. In the center was a lovely photograph of my grandmother in healthier days. This simple gathering has become a treasured memory.

Aside from making funeral arrangements, a number of other details need to be addressed. Did your loved one have a Will or Trust? Unfortunately, death in our society is usually followed by a flurry of formalities that can take many months to process and finalize. Tackling these tasks can sometimes impede our ability to grieve in peace but do the best you can in acknowledging your own needs.

Below, is a brief list of businesses you may need to inform of your loved one's passing:

- o Utility companies
- o Bank
- o Health and Life insurance companies
- o Post Office
- o Pension/ Retirement company

- Car insurance company
- Mortgage company
- Veteran's agency
- Credit card company

If possible, make a detailed contact list ahead of time, one that's specific to your loved one. Also, be sure to have several copies of the death certificate on hand. Let family members support you in taking care of these matters if they're legally authorized to do so.

Another errand awaiting you involves your loved one's unused medications. Don't throw them away or flush them down the toilet. Return them to your loved one's pharmacist in order for them to be properly disposed of.

The Loss of Your Caregiving Job

Your loved one's passing heralds the loss of your occupation as his or her caregiver. It's as if our caregiver uniform and ID badge (if we had one) were handed in at the pearly gates when we walked our loved one Home. We weren't fired, we didn't resign. Yet we're supposed to be something else now, but what? Although we had a life prior to caregiving, it may feel as though caregiving is all we know. It's who we are, who we became, whether we had wanted the job or not. Our bodies and minds have been burned to ash in caregiving's crucible. Now, without instructions, we must rise like the mythological Phoenix and live as a new creature.

The profound loss experienced after your loved one's passing may run deep. Your loved one shared their powerlessness with you in a manner reflecting your own future should you become ill, old, disabled, or in some other way, vulnerable. The bond formed between you both was highly personal. In all likelihood, he or she had never received this level of physical and emotional care since childhood. Being bathed, toileted, and fed were activities their mothers did for them. In certain respects, your loved one became child-like in his or her dependence upon you, while you as their caregiver become a nurturing figure for them. There's an emotional closeness that forms under these circumstances and as the reality of life's end draws near.

Channel the knowledge, experience, and compassion gained from your former caregiving days towards everyone you meet, especially those who are helpless. Ensuring that the vulnerable among us are respectfully cared for is ingrained in you now and certainly this world needs more kindness. But don't overlook yourself in doing so. You have time for yourself at this juncture and your loved one would want you to recover your mental and physical strength.

After my grandmother died, I found myself gravitating towards elderly people or anyone who appeared susceptible to the harsher aspects of this world. My lonely eyes searched for these folks as a hungry hawk might search for a rabbit – "Can I hold the door open for you?" "Can I reach that for you?" "Can I help you onto the bus?" It was difficult to turn the caregiver role off. Perhaps we never do. I missed caring for my grandmother. Looking after her was the most difficult thing I had ever done but I'd become accustomed to it. For a time, caregiving was all I knew or seemed to remember and letting go of that role didn't come easy.

I was surprised at how much I missed my grandmother's body after she passed away. I thought I'd only pine for what was on the inside – her kindness, good humor, and gentleness. But I had cared for her body for so long that I was missing it as well. In fact, moments after Nana died, I gently pulled up the blue blankets and bedsheet from the foot of her bed so that I could look at her lower legs and socked feet one more time. I frequently rubbed lotion on her legs and feet when she was alive. She always enjoyed it! I'd also soak her feet in a tub of warm water before cutting her nails for her. I wanted to see those legs and feet and tenderly run my hands over them one last time. I knew every detail about them – every freckle and scar, and I would miss caring for them.

Initially, I was unable to sleep throughout the night following Nana's passing. Accepting the fact that I was no longer 'on duty' wasn't easy. With no bedside bell ringing, my nights were heavy with silence. I no longer knew what to do with myself. The free time I now possessed, filled me with emptiness. Frequently, I awoke in tears, reliving parts of my caregiving experiences.

You too will mourn the loss of caring for your loved one. Be patient and gentle with yourself. As hard as it may be, you will make it through these early days, weeks, and months of bereavement.

Whenever sorrow comes,
Be kind to it.
For God has placed a
Pearl in sorrow's hand.

Rumi

Your Loved One's Belongings

Depending upon your circumstances, decisions need to be made regarding your loved one's belongings. Items may need to be sorted according to whether they'll be kept, donated, or discarded. These heart-breaking decisions can bring additional grief.

Prior to discarding or donating an object, consider mentally thanking it for the many years it gave your loved one. Doing so can assist you in letting go, especially if circumstances require you to release many more items than you would like. For example, "Thank you for keeping him or her protected from the rain," "…warm in the winter," or "…for putting a smile on his or her face." Sometimes, an entire house must be sold, perhaps an old family home filled with many memories. Expressing gratitude can help ease the pain of releasing it.

Consider taking photographs of certain items that you might wish to remember. Here's a silly example: my grandmother was the proud owner of an old washing machine with a mind of its own. It was a real clunker! It shook like an active volcano and made ominous sounds that threatened an eruption of sudsy lava! My grandmother always hoped the washing machine would out-survive her so that she wouldn't need to invest in a new one. The worst noise the machine made always occurred at the very end of the washing cycle. The metal behemoth made a tremendously loud *bang* that woke the dead and gave heart attacks to the living! The machine was located in Nana's bathroom. If you were unfortunate enough to be sitting on the toilet seat at the time of the supersonic boom, constipation issues were cured in a milli-second! I dreaded going to the bathroom whenever the washing machine was on. I never got used to that thunderous sound. But after Nana passed, I found myself surprisingly saddened at having to say good-bye to the rogue rattle-trap. Over the years, it had been the source of many family jokes. I shocked myself by actually taking a photo of it! Although the image isn't framed and hanging on my wall, I can look at the picture any time and enjoy a good laugh.

Hopefully, family and friends can help you sort your loved one's belongings. My sister Shannon left her own family in the U.S. and flew to Sydney to help my aunt and I empty Nana's house. This upsetting task could not have been accomplished without her assistance. Shannon helped sort items into categories: objects to be donated, discarded, or kept as remembrances. Periodically, we stretched our legs with long walks to give our emotions a break, especially from decisions regarding Nana's more personal belongings.

A few of my grandmother's close neighbors took unwanted objects off our hands. One woman took Nana's large plastic pill dispenser that I'd used to organize her medications. When the neighbor walked away with it, sadness suddenly washed over me and I was tempted to shout after her, "No wait, I can't give that up yet." I surprised myself at the attachment I felt to a simple plastic container. Afterwards, I realized the dispenser was a symbol; a reminder of the journey I had taken with my grandmother.

Workers from the palliative care hospital stopped by to pick up medical equipment they had loaned us. It was especially upsetting watching Nana's little red walker being folded and placed into the back of their station wagon. She had used it daily, especially enjoying short strolls to look at flowers and birds when the weather was nice.

You too, will feel warm tears flow down your cheeks when returning pieces of medical equipment that made every day caregiving easier in addition to sorting all the many personal objects belonging to your loved one. Remember, you're not alone in wading through these heart-wrenching waters. Many caregivers and their families have passed through them or are currently doing so. Feel their collective presence supporting you.

Closing the Door

If a much-loved family home with years of memories needs to be sold or otherwise vacated, stress and grief intermix. Closing the door to a familiar home for the final time and locking it with a well-worn key is a poignant moment. If possible, don't do this alone. Have someone accompany you.

Gently closing the front door to Nana's empty house for the last time felt surreal. My aunt and I thanked the home for the wonderful years my grandmother had enjoyed there and for the many memories our entire family had shared. Walking away, it was hard not to look behind us. But we didn't. My aunt and I decided we were going to face the direction in which we were moving. We were moving towards a new life, albeit without the one we so dearly loved. But we knew Nana's presence would always remain with us.

To everything there is a season
And a time to every purpose under heaven –

A time to be born and a time to die,
... A time to weep and a time to laugh,
A time to mourn and a time to dance.

Ecclesiastes

Engage in Activities

Slowly but surely, begin engaging in activities that are meaningful to you. Undoubtedly there were many things you were unable to do while caregiving. Now you can pick up a former hobby or pursue a new area of interest. Find something healing. Personally, I found writing poetry about my caregiving experiences helpful but writing is a solitary activity. I knew I also needed to mix with people again and hear other stories aside from my own. While engaging in small talk with others might not sound appealing, you do need people in your life. Most individuals have been touched by grief and will gladly share their own experiences with you. Listen to these folks and let them support you. Remind yourself that you're not alone in living through loss. Join in solidarity with the millions of people around the world currently shedding tears for someone they deeply miss.

Browse your community newspaper to find classes such as painting, aerobics, or quilting. Join a gardening club or volunteer an hour or two each week at a charitable organization. There are countless activities available in most communities. Find something that 'calls your name.'

In particular, spend as much time as possible in the great outdoors. Reap the unique benefits of sunshine, fresh air, and long walks. Quiet time in the natural world can be especially healing to your aching spirit. Although plants and animals also die, nature is replete with growth and full of the overcoming of obstacles. Let nature inspire you to live in the present moment – the only moment in which true healing can take place and in which peace can cradle your sorrow.

Caregiving leaves its mark on us.
No matter what we do to prepare ourselves
the hole left behind looms large.

Dale L. Baker

Caregiver Post-Traumatic Stress Disorder

Exposure to extremely stressful experiences may result in some caregivers developing PTSD. Affected caregivers may not become aware of the disorder until after their loved one has died, finding themselves left with feelings of anxiety, anguish, or numbness. While grieving, individuals with PTSD may relive certain experiences characterized by intrusive flashbacks for months or years.

Following Nana's passing, I frequently experienced unpleasant flashbacks. I wasn't expecting them and their sudden appearance took me by surprise. Troubled, I mentioned these flashbacks to my bereavement counselor. She told me they weren't uncommon; a civilian PTSD for which caregivers were at risk. Recurring images of my grandmother dying in hospital and the final evening she spent at her home when paramedics were called, appeared upon the inner screen of my mind. In addition, I experienced flashbacks revolving around Nana's many hospitalizations. These involved my proximity to dying patients, grieving families, and witnessing the deceased being wheeled from their rooms. Struggling to reconcile these images and the strong feelings they invoked, with my new life was challenging.

Intrusive flashbacks occurred day and night but especially during quiet moments. I knew there was nowhere to hide and no escape. Symptoms went wherever I did. The flashbacks, I hoped, would ease with the passage of time. They were frequent the first year following Nana's passing and slowly decreased after that. Occasionally, I still experience them.

Whenever a flashback intrudes upon my mind, I acknowledge it and then let it go, even though the emotions stirred up are powerful. I choose to think of these images as puffy white clouds being blown across the inner sky of my mind. Instead of resisting them or fighting them off, I allow them to drift by in their own time. Seek out bereavement counseling or other forms of therapeutic assistance if you too suffer flashbacks, anxiety, numbness, detachment, or nightmares following your loved one's passing. Don't try to suffer through PTSD alone.

The wound is the place
Where the light enters you.

Rumi

Caregiver Guilt

Aside from PTSD, caregivers can also suffer guilt. Following a period of much-needed rest, I found myself having second thoughts regarding how good a caregiver I was. Rethinking decisions I'd made filled me with self-doubt. Did I take over too many tasks from Nana too soon? Could I have been more understanding? Did I do everything I could to ease my grandmother's end-of-life burden? Could I have spent more quality time with her? Could I have thought more about what she was going through rather than what I was going through? These were some of the questions I asked myself.

We become more reflective once our loved one passes away. Better rested and better fed, we may decide our caregiving skills fell short. Yet, if we recall the enormous fatigue and stress that enveloped us, we realize we did our best under trying circumstances. Berating ourselves with "If only ..." serves no useful purpose. Should we find ourselves as caregivers again in the future, we'll enter the new situation with our eyes fully open and a wealth of experiences beneath our belts.

Don't be hard on yourself if you feel you could have done better as a caregiver. Each of us has 20/20 vision in hindsight.

Upon life's journey, we learn as we go – every last one of us. Learn from the past and forgive yourself if need be. But know that you did something wonderful for your loved one. You can be proud of that. As a caregiver, you were a god-send for him or her.

Reminders of Death

After being the caregiver of a loved one with terminal illness, you may long for a break from death and dying before fully facing the world again. Death has become much more real for you as a result of your experiences and taking a break from it can help. But sometimes life has other plans and death can be hard to avoid, even for a short period of time.

A month or so following my grandmother's passing, I boarded a small whale watching vessel in Sydney Harbour. I felt the need to do something different and experience a change of scenery. The wild wind in my hair, the rolling motion of the boat, and sparkling sunshine upon the blue sea were a healing balm for my grief. It was lovely to escape the darker side of loss. I was thrilled as several female humpback whales and their calves swam within sight of our boat. I marveled at how enormous and amazingly beautiful these gentle giants were. The females were taking their little ones south to the krill-laden waters of Antarctica for the summer. Strong currents along Australia's eastern coast carried them upon a watery 'conveyor-belt' that generations of whales had taken. I wanted to go with them. The spaciousness of sky and sea was soothing and transformative. The car-sized calves reminded me of new life, new beginnings.

On the return trip back to Sydney Harbour, I stood at the rail on the opposite side of the boat. The undulating coastline was riddled with lovely beaches and expensive homes. In other places, the landscape was rugged with tall, weathered sandstone cliffs. Harsh surf pounded the stony walls, exploding into powerful sprays at the base of dark, drenched rocks. Watching the incredible scenery speed by, I suddenly did a double-take. There on top of one of the cliffs was an old cemetery. From my vantage point on the boat, the ancient grey tombstones resembled dead people from a horror film standing up and looking out to sea; looking at me. I felt a horrible sick feeling in the pit of my stomach. I couldn't escape the reminder of death. My disturbing thoughts at unexpectedly seeing the cemetery, spoke volumes in regards to my PTSD and continued need for healing. I'd experienced a few hours observing humpback mothers and their young, forgetting that even for them the yearly migration is wrought with peril.

Death is an ever-present and essential component of life. In the acceptance of that indisputable fact lies deep inner peace. If possible, take gentle, baby steps in de-sensitizing yourself while remaining aware that death doesn't always wait patiently for us to undergo a period of rest and recovery. Seek assistance if you need it and remember, you aren't alone.

When it seems that our sorrow
Is too great to be borne,
Let us think of the great family
Of the heavy hearted
Into which our grief has given us
Entrance, and inevitably,
We will feel about us their arms,
Their sympathy, their understanding.

Helen Keller

A String of Pearls

While grieving, you may notice that the passing of your loved one has triggered memories of other losses such as that of other family members, friends, or pets who are now gone. Death is similar to a string of pearls. Each person who dies is another pearl added. Although each passing is unique, the pearls are connected by the same string and each new death reconnects us with the others. Be gentle with yourself as you wrap this string of pearls around your heart. Allow it to support you and bind your wounds rather than weigh you down. Cherish each precious pearl and honor the loved one it represents by fully living the rest of your days.

Reminders of Caregiving

Many reminders of your caregiving days await you. Memories may be triggered by a song, fragrance, book cover, or a million other things. Some memories will make you chuckle while others will wash your face in tears. Embrace whatever comes along. Your journey as a caregiver by your loved one's side was a true adventure. Take these opportunities to remember, process, and heal.

As mentioned in an earlier chapter, trips to the supermarket were vacation time for me while caregiving. But after Nana died, that changed. Instead, I noticed items on the shelves that I'd purchased for her such as anti-rash cream, baby wipes, and her favorite candies. I missed no longer needing to buy them. You too, will find it's almost impossible to go anywhere without reminders of caregiving. It's alright to feel whatever comes to you.

Five months after Nana passed away, I was walking through an outdoor market back in the Arizona desert and thinking of my grandmother. It was hard not to. My days were filled with missing her. Suddenly over the speaker system, the Hollies 1969 song, *He Ain't Heavy, He's My Brother* began playing. I lost it. I couldn't stop or hide the tears. The lyrics reminded me of caregiving; of holding hands, soft hugs, and comforting kisses. Despite the many hardships of caring for my grandmother at the end of her life, the moment I heard that song, Nana didn't seem so heavy and I would have carried her all over again.

If I had a flower for
Every time I thought of you,
I could walk in my garden forever.

Alfred Lord Tennyson

Conversation Starters

From Caregiver to Caregiver, What I Want You to Know:

~ You may experience the loss of your loved one in a different way than those who were not their caregiver due to the intimacy built during the course of his or her illness. Celebrate the memory of that closeness by taking care of yourself.

~ You'll need time to mentally process all that you've been through. Sometimes our brains struggle to comprehend everything that has transpired. You've been on a difficult journey and need to fully grasp the many twists and turns you experienced along the way. With time, you'll come to accept the path's completion and its impact upon you.

~ You've lost your caregiving job and following a period of deep rest you'll need to decide what to do with your life going forward. What will you do that honors your loved one's memory? What gives you a sense of continued purpose? Poet Mary Oliver once wrote, "Tell me, what do you plan to do with your one wild and precious life?" The answer to this question quietly awaits you.

~ No-one leaves this world without experiencing some form of loss. Never feel embarrassed or ashamed of your tears. You've earned them. The moist and tender tracks they leave upon your face signify that you have loved someone.

In closing, you've been a caregiver and walked your loved one Home. Now it's time for you to rest and wrap yourself in a blanket of tenderness. Be your own caregiver and as each night falls, close your eyes in peace, knowing you did well. The hand-off is complete. Your loved one is now in the care of the angels.

Hope is the thing with feathers
That perches in the soul -
and sings the tune without the words
And never stops at all.

Emily Dickinson

He Ain't Heavy, He's My Brother

*The road is long
With many a winding turn
That leads us to who knows where
Who knows where
But I'm strong
Strong enough to carry him
He ain't heavy, he's my brother
So on we go
His welfare is of my concern
No burden is he to bear
We'll get there
For I know
He would not encumber me
He ain't heavy, he's my brother
If I'm laden at all
I'm laden with sadness
That everyone's heart
Isn't filled with the gladness
Of love for one another
It's a long, long road
From which there is no return
While we're on the way to there
Why not share
And the load
Doesn't weigh me down at all
He ain't heavy he's my brother,
He ain't heavy, he's my brother.*

The Hollies
Songwriters: Bob Russell and Bobby Scott (1969)

Conclusion

*The number one thing caregivers
Can do for other caregivers
Is to say, "You are not alone."*

Author Unknown

How should a book on caregiving end? What parting words can point like a street sign to a quiet inner sanctuary where encouragement abounds, sadness is understood, and wounds are healed? Caring for a terminally ill loved one is a labor of love heavy with responsibility. It's one of the most emotionally, spiritually, and physically difficult excursions a person can undertake. When the journey is finally completed, we do not rest in peaceful leisure but are left with grief, flashbacks, and quite often guilt; second-guesses at what we might have done differently or better. We are fallible and imperfect after all, learning more from our mistakes than our successes; mere humans trying to do a superhuman task. But that's where love comes in. Not a weak, sappy, or frail love but a strong, willful, and powerful tide that pushes us forward when we think we can no longer go on; when we feel too tired to do one more thing. But we must also uplift and cradle ourselves using that very same force. We must love ourselves for doing a difficult job the best way we knew how. We will learn from our challenging experiences and grow stronger because of them. We will support and encourage one another as fellow caregivers.

    Although my long days and nights of caring for Nana are over, I think of them often. Caregiving changed me. I now look at life through a wide-angle lens, viewing the larger picture. As for my grandmother - her memory and presence are with me always, inseparable as my shadow whenever I walk beneath warm sunlight. Being her caregiver was the most meaningful thing I have ever done or will likely ever do. I can think of no other worthy accomplishment that would exceed being a caregiver for someone so dear. I hope caregiving is the same for you. May God bless you as you walk your loved one Home.

A Prayer for the Caregiver

Unknown and often unnoticed,
You are a hero nevertheless.
For your love, sacrificial, is God at his best.
You walk by faith in the darkness of the great unknown,
And your courage, even in weakness,
Gives life to your beloved.
You hold shaky hands and provide the ultimate care:
Your presence, the knowing,
That you are simply there.
You rise to face the giant of disease and despair,
It is your finest hour, though you may be unaware.
You are resilient, amazing and beauty excelled,
You are the caregiver and you have done well!

Bruce McIntyre

Acknowledgements

Writing a book for caregivers of the terminally ill has been cathartic, challenging, and rewarding. I especially wish to thank my mother for her endless support and encouragement as I worked through the ups and downs of writing a book of this nature. To each member of my family: a lovable motley bunch on both sides of the Pacific, my heartfelt thanks for sustaining me upon the journey of walking Nana Home. In Australia, I would like to thank Aunt Sharon, who lost her husband a year before she lost her mother and whose constant prayers, weekly visits, and daily phone calls were appreciated. We logged in many hours at the hospital together including Nana's long end-of-life vigil. It wasn't easy but we made it! Special appreciation extends to Brenda & Robert, Jennifer, Lorna, Valerie, and Stephen. To my cousin Kim, thank you for sharing hard-earned insights. You were a great source of information and consolation. In America, my heartfelt appreciation to my sisters Renee and Shannon who endured long flights to Sydney in order to help where they could. I can't begin to tell you how much of a difference your presence made. Renee, thank you for completely taking over meal time from morning to night. You walked long distances for Nana's favorite fruits and were able to prepare meals she actually enjoyed. I loved them too! Thank you for all the many laughs you gave Nana as you played cards, read magazines together, and chatted day and night. You gave her much happiness at the end of her life and when in the States, Nana loved the many cards you mailed to her. You have my gratitude always! Shannon, thank you for helping clear Nana's home after she passed. It was a sad task that could not have been completed without you. Thank you for keeping me company during that difficult time, especially for the long consoling walks and watching episodes of *Skippy* at 3 am when neither one of us could sleep! I am truly grateful for your kindness and assistance. What wonderful sisters I have! For dear Mum & Dad who were heart-broken at not being able to travel to Australia during Nana's illness, I thank you for your daily prayers, phone calls, letters, gift packages, emails of support, and for looking after my pets: Scotty and Dundee. You were definitely with Nana and I in spirit. We knew it and were stronger for it. Love can and does travel around the world, even when our bodies cannot.

A special word of thanks to friends and neighbors along Whitegates Ave and beyond, including Betty, Alf, Mick, Big Joyce, Bob, Evelyn, Roma, Irene, and Elizabeth & Bruce. In giving thanks, I'd be remiss to overlook my furry friend Chee Chee, the neighborhood cat and connoisseur of fine scraps of chicken, who lifted my spirits countless times when I missed my pets back in America.

Caring for the needs of a terminally ill person involves a team of hardworking individuals. Special thanks go to Nana's longtime GP, Dr. Elton Chen and his associate Mingga Anggawa. In particular, I am deeply indebted to the wonderful nurses at Nurses on Wheels, Bexley, for support which far exceeded their duties as community nurses. You taught me, supported me, and treated my grandmother with the utmost kindness and dignity. For that, my family and I will always be grateful. In particular, I would like to thank these remarkable nurses: Richelle Sheehan, Shirley Fulham, Lynn Laurie, Rhonda Dundas, Narelle Hofma, and Wendy.

Nana's final year was marked by repeated admissions into Calvary Hospital, Kogarah, where she was under the care of a small army of dedicated people. My deep appreciation to Dr. Caitlyn Sheehan, Dr. Margaret Rainbird, Mary Ashton, Robyn Martin, Jane Hogan, Angela Heathwood, Nicola Ross, Fran Stewart, as well as Anne-Marie Traynor and her amazing team of volunteers. Three of you in particular, spent a great deal of time with Nana and I while we were upon this journey: Carmel Higgins, Kathleen Hossack, and Kate Holdsworth. You were confidants, comforters, and teachers for us and I will always remember your names. Thank you so much.

Recommended Reading

Annesley, Mike. *Practical Mindfulness: A Step-by-Step Guide.* Cons. Ken A. Verni. London: Dorling Kindersley, 2015.

Babcock, Elise NeeDell. *When Life Becomes Precious: A Guide for Loved Ones and Friends of Cancer Patients.* New York: Bantam, 1997.

Brennan, Frank. *Standing at the Platform: Stories and Reflections from Palliative Care.* Kogarah: Calvary Health Care, 2011.

Cooper, Torie. *Laying Nana Down: Poems of Caregiving and Loss.* San Bernardino: Blue Wattle Press, 2017.

Cotner, June. *Back to Joy: Little Reminders to Help Us Through Tough Times.* Kansas City: Andrews McMeel, 2014.

Cotner, June. *Serenity Prayers: Prayers, Poems, and Prose to Soothe Your Soul.* Kansas City: Andrews McMeel, 2014.

Guntzelman, Joan, and Lou Guntzelman. *Come Healing God: Prayers During Illness.* 2nd ed. Liguori: Liguori, 2004.

Hickman, Martha Whitmore. *Healing After Loss: Daily Meditations for Working Through Grief.* 2nd ed. New York: HarperCollins, 2002.

Murphy, Betsy. *Guide to Caregiving in the Final Months of Life.* Middleburg: TM Brown, 2007.

Nicoll, David, and Sandy Heinisch. *Lights for Dark Places.* Brentwood: BAEB, 2010.

Normile, Patti. *Prayers for Caregivers.* 2nd ed. St. Meinrad: Abbey Press, 2014.

Nouwen, Henri J.M. *A Spirituality of Caregiving.* Nashville: Upper Room, 2011.

Orsborn, Carol. *The Art of Resilience: 100 Paths to Wisdom and Strength in an Uncertain World.* New York: Three Rivers Press, 1997.

Staudacher, Carol. *A Time to Grieve: Meditations for Healing After the Death of a Loved One.* New York: HarperOne, 1994.

Index

advanced directives, 43-44
    Do Not Resuscitate order, 44
    final wishes, 45

bathroom supplies, 40-42
bedsores, 88
bereavement services, 174
beverages, 42, 104-105

choking/coughing issues, 42, 113
cognitive issues, 39, 81-83
comfort care, 158
communication, 28-29, 59-60, 120-121
community nursing services, 121-122, 149
control concerns (quality of life), 91-92
Conversations Starters, 70, 95, 111, 128, 150, 174, 194

death, 79-80, 139, 166-167
Death Certificate, 183
depression, 22, 79-80
disposable underwear, 40-41

emotions, 21-23, 52-54, 68, 156
    anger, 21-22
    frustration, 55-56, 68
    guilt, 66, 190-191
    sadness/sorrow, 92, 136-137

enjoyment/entertainment, 45-47, 90-91, 108, 112, 140-141

final words, 162-163
funeral arrangements, 182
       food issues, 42-43, 85-87, 96, 104-105, 111, 113

grief, 179-181, 192-193
       anticipatory grief, 20-22, 63-64

hospital admissions, 135-138, 147-148
       discharge, 145-146, 149
humor, 34, 68, 93-94, 145, 164

incontinence, 40

legal considerations, 43-44

medical equipment, 38, 130
medications, 24, 35-37,
       disposal of, 183
medical alert device, 149
mindfulness, 33
mistakes, 23, 58-59
monitoring your loved one, 25, 38, 88-89

nature, 67, 188
nausea, 42
Nursing Homes, 29-30, 131-132, 142-143

occasions (holidays, birthdays), 47, 92-93, 94
Occupational Therapists, 38, 57, 124

pain, 29, 37
Palliative Care, 122
Paramedics, 125
Pastoral Care, 32, 80, 124, 159
pets, 148

PTSD, 189-190,
Practical Tips, 35, 66, 94, 146

relationship issues, 27-28, 55-56, 80-81, 105-108
respite, 26-27, 103, 115, 130, 138-139
routine, 32-33, 97

safety concerns, 39, 72 ,83
sleep deprivation, 24-25, 57
Social Workers, 29, 123, 142
spiritual considerations, 32, 80, 87
stress, 21, 52-54, 56, 131

Volunteers, 124, 161-162

well-being (of caregiver), 67-69, 159

Permissions and Acknowledgements

Grateful acknowledgement is made to the authors and publishers of the following material. Every effort has been made to contact the original sources. If notified, the author will be pleased to rectify an omission in future editions.

Dale L. Baker for "Caregiving leaves its mark . . ." from *More Than I Could Ever Know: How I Survived Caregiving.* Copyright © 2014. Published by MsDale Publishing. msdalelbaker@gmail.com
Sheila Cassidy for "The world is not divided . . ." from *Audacity to Believe.* Copyright © 1978. Published by Darton, Longman & Todd.
Molly Friedenfeld for "If someone is facing . . ." from *The Book of Simple Truths.* Copyright © 2013. Published by She Writes Press. www.mollyfriedenfeld.com
He Ain't Heavy, He's My Brother
Words and Music by Bob Russell and Bobby Scott
Copyright (c) 1969 Music Sales Corporation and Jenny Music
Copyright Renewed
International Copyright Secured   All Rights Reserved
Reprinted by Permission of Hal Leonard LLC

Helen Keller for "When it seems that our sorrow . . ." Copyright © American Foundation for the Blind, Helen Keller Archive.

Bruce McIntyre for the poem *"A Prayer for the Caregiver."* www.brucemcintyre.com

Kitty Tsui for "I'm a flower Poa . . ." from *The Words of a Woman Who Breathes Fire.* Copyright © 1983. Published by Bella Books.

The Author with her Grandmother

About the Author

Australian-American author Torie Cooper was the sole caregiver for her beloved grandmother in Sydney, Australia. *Love, Laughter, and Morphine: A Compassionate Guide for Caregivers of the Terminally Ill*, is Torie's first work of non-fiction. While writing this book, she took continuing education coursework from CSU's Institute of Palliative Care. Torie has written two collections of poetry - *Laying Nana Down: Poems of Caregiving and Loss* and *Nature: A Collection of Poems*. Torie divides her time among family and friends on both sides of the Pacific Ocean.

Notes

www.ingramcontent.com/pod-product-compliance
Lightning Source LLC
Chambersburg PA
CBHW031639040426
42453CB00006B/158